"Life is just a series of decisions we have the opportunity to make. If you want a better quality of life, get better at making decisions."

— Dr. Guinevere Anne Stasio

Book Layout © Million-Dollar-Author 2021

Pivot to Purpose. -- 1st edition.

ISBN: 978-0-6450943-0-5

Introduction

Do you ever remember sitting in class, feeling you knew the answer, but not feeling confident enough to raise your hand?

Still feeling the rattle from the cobblestone streets of Boston, the Oola Dream Tour rolled into the sleepy suburb of Waltham, MA. We had noticed we had become a culture of distractions, losing sight of our dreams. Our mission was simple: reconnect people to their dreams. Our crazy idea was to collect one million hand-written dreams on stickers on the side of our 1970 VW surf bus. We figured if someone reconnects to their dream and made it happen, not only would their life become better, but they would inspire those they love to do the same, and in this way, we could change the world.

We were invited to speak at an event to share our message of creating your dream life by teaching people how to stop living by default, and start living life by design.

We had just launched a new book and asked for volunteers to sell books at a small back table at the event. Gwen raised her hand.

Her compensation was simply a free ticket to the event, a signed book and a sincere dose of gratitude. But it turned out to be so much more. You see, it turns out, she didn't just raise her hand to sell books. Looking back to that day, she raised her hand to change; to find the courage to pivot in the direction of the way she wanted to live, and away from the way she thought she had to live … it was that day she made the pivot toward purpose. This book is a real-life example of the power of raising your hand. The ripple effect of finding the courage to raise your hand in the face of self-doubt and the unknown. Learning to listen to that little voice inside that is pulling you toward your purpose, and away from safe, stressful, and unfulfilling.

Now it is your turn. By turning the pages of this book you are raising your hand. Saying yes to positive change. Saying yes to life by design. Saying yes to living life fully.

It is all here. Gwen will walk you step by step, to overcome what is getting in the way, see clearly the pivot you need to make, and most importantly show you how to get there. She knows, because this is her story, and as a successful life coach, she has guided countless people on the journey you are about to partake in.

You are designed for a purpose. Contained within these pages is the path. Congratulations on raising your hand. Turn the page and let your adventure begin ...

Dr. Dave Braun and Dr. Troy Amdahl
"The Oola Guys"
International Best Selling Authors

Acknowledgements

I want to take a minute to thank my husband Adam for having the balls to ask me the one question that truly got me thinking about my life and what I wanted to get out of it. And for always loving me so hard and teaching me how to love in return.

I also want to thank my work wife Rosy for always encouraging me to go for it, and Danielle for sharing your pivot to purpose story with me and with the readers of this book.

And of course, I want to thank my sister who is my built-in best friend, the one I can count on to give it to me straight and always make me laugh. Without you, I wouldn't be who I am.

Thank you to my parents for supporting me in my ideas and business adventures, even if you weren't sure they would work out.

And last but not least, thank you Rhiannon and Jolene for allowing me to be a kid again and have more fun.

Getting help

Before you even start this book, I want to give you a gift.

For everyone that purchases this book I have some resources that will help you pivot to your own ideal life.

You can access them here.

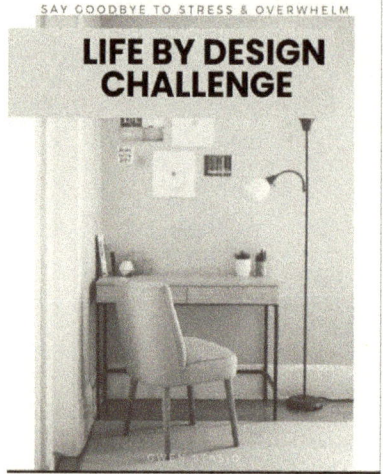

SAY GOODBYE TO STRESS & OVERWHELM

LIFE BY DESIGN CHALLENGE

https://roilhighness.com/landing/life-by-design-landing-page

About the Author

Dr. Guinevere Stasio, the author of Pivot to Purpose, is devoted to helping women design their dream life. She is designed by nature to pull resources, people and opportunities in so that she can master them and then turn around and teach them to others.

What began as a mission to find balance and fulfillment in her own life, became a movement teaching woman how to regain control of the time they are given and unlock their wildest dreams.

Gwen is great at processing data, being mentally creative and inspiring others to think. She's also really great at handstands and never misses an opportunity to flip her world upside down.

She is a mom, Doctor of Audiology, Certified Aromatherapist, and Oola Life + Financial coach who will tell you that many of life's answers can be found at the beach.

She lives and continues to write and coach in New Hampshire, with her two daughter's Jolene and Rhiannon, and her husband Adam.

Gwen loves to hear from readers. Visit her website at http://www.roilhighness.com

CONTENTS

Chapter One

ALTERNATIVES

It's Time to Start Looking at Alternatives

As with all things "new mom" related, I was used to being blindsided. But the phone call I just received was more than that; it was a blindsided gut punch. The kind that leaves you with that gutteral "ugh" afterwards.

I was sitting in my living room and had just finished feeding my five-week-old baby. As any new mom, I was completely flustered with simply

19

trying to figure out this new mom life when my phone rang. It was my boss. I hadn't talked to him since the birth of my baby, a few days before I went on unpaid maternity leave. I assumed he was calling to check-in and confirm the date of my return to the office. I was not expecting the verbal bomb that was dropped on me that day. He was calling to let me know that he had evaluated my pay and decided that he would no longer be able to pay me what I was making before I went on leave. He was cutting my pay by $15,000.

To be completely honest, I had no words. I sat there for a second and tried to comprehend what he was telling me, knowing that I was going to have to go back in just a week, knowing that I had just signed my five-week-old baby up for daycare with people that I barely knew, knowing that I was going to have to pay for that daycare, and knowing that I didn't have any other option. I felt the lump in my throat forming. I was numb.

I truly enjoyed going to work. I loved helping people hear! But in that moment I felt taken aback, taken advantage of, and just not supported or considered. It felt like all the work I had done had gone unnoticed. I ended the phone call with a "I guess I'll see you in a week." and then just let it all out.

∾

We thought we had it all figured out … until we didn't.

∾

My head felt like it was 10 feet from my body. I never expected that that could even happen to me.

Eight years in school with a doctorate and a respected position in an office where my role is necessary to keep the office flowing to figure out that I was not in control of my income. I cried. I know my hormones were everywhere at that point. I turned to my husband and I told him exactly what had happened on the call and he was in just as much disbelief as I was. How can this happen? How can that just be pulled out from under me without any warning signs? We were both pretty upset, unsure what to do in that moment except continue on and do what I was expected to; go do my job.

I received my Doctorate of Audiology in 2010. I loved helping people figure out their hearing and helping them get hearing aids. To watch someone gain a new perspective on life by getting some hearing back or hearing for the first time was really a joyful part of my day. I had worked in a hospital setting, in an Audiologist's private practice and finally in this last position in conjunction with an Ear Nose and Throat Doctor. This was the way I envisioned a career in Audiology; the collaboration of two professionals working together to help people with their sense of hearing. We both knew we needed each other and couldn't do our jobs without one another. I needed his services so that he could help me with diagnoses on my patients, and he needed my services so that I could test his patients and let him know what was going on with their hearing. It was a collaborative workplace that also gave me the freedom to run the audiology side of the practice myself.

Right before I got pregnant with my first baby, my husband realized that he was not working his dream job. He decided to switch careers from being a union carpenter to becoming a firefighter. In fact, the second night in the hospital after I had my first baby, he couldn't even stay with me because he had an important firefighter test the next day. We had multiple conversations about him changing his career; to do it, or not to do it. It was scary because he had only known union carpentry and he was really good at what he did. Plus, he made really good money in the union. But he wasn't happy.

The switch from carpenter to firefighter meant a 50% pay cut. Oof. But we were prepared. Making adjustments to our lifestyle and knowing that my salary was consistent we decided that life was short and it was important for him to love his job. We thought we had it all figured it out, until we didn't.

Chapter Two

PIVOT IS THE NEW BUZZWORD ...

... Because That's What We Need Right Now

Despite all this, we had made the decision that it would be okay for him to pivot to this new job. Above all else, I wanted him to be completely happy in what he was doing, and he was certainly not happy in the job he was in. He was getting up at three o'clock in the morning, driving an hour to work, working eight to ten hours, then driving back home for an hour. It just wasn't the best life for him or for us.

When I walked in the doors to the office, everyone was excited about me being back. But I also knew that dreaded in person conversation was coming with my boss.

After I put away the 6,000 bags that every new mom has to lug to to work, my boss came in to chat. He had a lot of reasons why he couldn't afford to pay me what I was making before maternity leave. While I was out he had decided to switch from being part of a hospital to now being a private practice, and for the first time looked at my salary. He hadn't realized how much I was making because he wasn't the one who had hired me in the first place, the hospital had.

There were a lot of tears that day. A lot of frustrations and emotions and just wondering how I would be able to feel like my time and role was respected. I felt frustrated that I wasn't being heard and that he would not entertain alternatives.

After a long first day back, I went home and evaluated what I enjoyed in my life. I watched my husband pivot and change his career at 30 years old. He was finally finding joy in his work. It felt impossible for me to pivot. After eight years of school and a ton of student loan debt, what would I even pivot to? This was all I'd known for eight years. And even though I didn't know exactly what I'd do, on that day in January of 2015 I began devising a plan to leave that job. In 2018 I did just that.

Shit Happens. Look for the Silver Lining

Life is funny if you're open to seeing it that way. Things happen to fall in your lap precisely when you need them. If this had landed in my lap at any other time in my life, I'm not sure I would have been awake enough to see it.

As I said before, I love helping people. With the birth of my new daughter, I started to explore healthier options for soaps and candles and all the things that could possibly come in contact with her. I was suddenly very aware of what I used in my home. Apparently, I wasn't the only one.

In March of 2015 I was introduced to essential oils. But it wasn't the first time I had seen them. My mother owned a soap making company when I was a kid and she used them to scent her soap. She also used to put a drop of lavender in the vacuum bag at home. But this time I saw them in a new light, a way to use them to live healthier, happier and simpler lives.

During this time of exploration, I got introduced to a group of women who were not only creating a healthier way of living for themselves, they were running a business helping others do the same. They were making their own hours, supporting and learning from each other, and in charge of their own income. I loved it so much I partnered with a company that provided people with natural resources for their body. I also decided to obtain my aromatherapy certification because I needed to know all the things. I grew fast, and I was still able to help people except now it was on my own terms.

I worked this job every hour I wasn't working at the office. The plan was to create an income that matched my office income so that I could leave my job. Passion, desire and determination got me there in 2018. I took my business home and never looked back.

One of the simplest things that I had always dreamed of doing but never saw it being a reality was to be able to wake up, have my coffee, and go to the gym in the morning. Working full time, I never thought that was possible. I was always baffled when I saw people at the gym at nine o'clock in the morning. I'd think "They must be nurses or doctors who work off hours and that's how they get to the gym in the morning." I never ever thought that was possible for me.

And now I have my gym in my basement. I get up in the morning and while my kids are eating breakfast, I go downstairs and work out on my time. There I am at 8am working out. One thing I never thought possible until my eyes were opened to possibilities. Now, I choose my work time, I choose my kid time, I choose my family time and I choose to have fun every day. I've created this flexibility, a career that allows me to do what I'm passionate about and a life I truly love. Something that once completely controlled me became the thing I had complete control over.

The Only Way to Get There is to Get There

I was 27 years old when I first heard the words "personal development". It wasn't taught in school. In fact, it's quite the opposite. From the age of five years old school says you learn a task, perform it and present it to your teacher and then your teacher says whether you did or didn't do well according to a standard. You do that every day, every year right through high school. You're constantly trying to meet the expectations that society sets up for you, constantly checking a box. They tell you to take algebra, pass the class, and move to the next subject. Take chemistry, pass the class, move to the next class. If you fail, you repeat until you meet the standards of the system. Never once do they take the individual interests of the student into account. You just keep moving through the system until you graduate, get a job, buy a house, get married, have kids and get a dog. Perfect life complete. Or is it? We are constantly chasing these expectations of society rather than being able to look out into the world and experience, explore and figure out what we want to do for ourselves.

So back to personal development. This is exactly what allowed me to see that I could dream for myself. It allowed me to grow my mindset for the first time. Personal development allowed me to see that I must learn how to connect with myself first, before I could learn how to be connected with the world. Those two pieces working together allowed me to figure out what my dreams were, who I truly was, what I'm meant to do here in this world, and to design my life around just that. Because the lesson is, you don't have to check the boxes that society tells you to, but they won't tell you that. That's why I'm writing this book.

So chances are if you picked up this book you're tired of going to a job you hate but feel you are stuck because well….#kids #bills and #life. You want to have more fun, you fear missing out on your kids life, you wonder if you should suck it up for 40 years at a job that pays the bills but you don't love or maybe you know you don't like how things are going but you're not really sure how to make the change or what to even do about it. You're ready for less stress, to stop feeling like you sold your soul to your job and like you need to take a vacation from your own life. Or maybe, you're the lucky young soul who hasn't graduated high school yet and your mom, dad, uncle, brother or sister bought this book for you because they know just how important it is to be in love with your life. And you probably won't listen to them, so they're hoping a total stranger will make a mark. Doesn't matter because you're here and this is where YOUR story starts.

Skeptics read this: if you are concerned it is too late to make a change, the answer is a resounding NO. It is never too late to design the life you desire. Napoleon Hill said "Those who succeed in an outstanding way seldom do so before the age of 40. More often, they do not strike their real pace until they are well beyond the age of 50." No matter where you are in life you can pivot, if you so desire. My guess is, you desire because you wouldn't be reading this book if you didn't.

In reading this book you now have the power in your hands to pass it on to the next generation too. So in some ways, it is also never too early to start designing the life you desire. If you are concerned you don't have the time to figure this out, consider what it will feel like taking your last few breaths wishing you had really lived. I want you yelling "YOLO!" on your way out, ok?

This book will show you that no matter what path you took up until now, anything is possible. Most people think success comes when you check all the boxes. I'm here to tell you that they are wrong, and there's a movement coming...it's actually already happening. I want you to be a part of it and you can just by reading this book and starting on your journey. Because what most people are missing is the confidence, the action steps and the belief that anything is possible. And that's exactly what you'll get by reading this book.

Chapter Three

FREEDOM

Time Freedom

Have you ever Google searched "time freedom"? There is a lot of content out there. What most people are looking for when they want to work towards time freedom is a step by step strategy that they can follow. And sure, in the overall scheme of things there's the equation of 'make or have more money so you can have more fun', right? But it's so much more than that. Anyone can work 100+ hours a week to make more money, but all they'll get is burnout and stress and bags under their eyes. Ask me how I know. It's not exactly the ideal time freedom equation.

There's something that has to happen first before we can create time freedom though, and that is dreaming. Not the eyes closed laying in bed (or if you're my husband, eyes closed standing, sitting or laying down) type of dreaming. I'm talking about daydreaming. I want people to learn that they can dream when they're wide awake. I want them to learn HOW to dream because somewhere along the way into adulthood, dreaming gets shoved to the side. As we step through certain parts of our life, we experience situations that limit our beliefs. Some of it's not on purpose. Actually most of it is accidental. But I want people to be able to realize that even as an adult, if they don't like where they are, they can dream a new life into existence. If they decide the reason why they're here on earth is to be a giraffe trainer, they have everything they need already to become a giraffe trainer. They have all the drive and desire inside of them to make that dream come true. They just have to learn how to access it, and then learn how to put it out into the world. Time freedom is enjoying your time while you're here, so if you can create a career and life that you fall in love with every day your feet hit the floor, you've done it right.

Sometimes we dream and we don't even realize it. When I saw people at the gym in the morning and longed to be them, I was dreaming. But I couldn't see it because I was so stuck on following the system that society layed out in front of me that I could only see that. I thought following the system would make me successful. And doesn't everyone want to be successful? I did want to make more money, but I also wanted to have more fun and spend more time with friends and family. I just thought all of that happened after you retire. What I slowly started to realize was that putting in 40 hours a week for 40 years just to get 40% of your pay when you retired, was not really all that enticing. What happens if you don't make it there? Because we always say things like, "I'll do that when I retire. I'll have more time when I retire." But what's the point of living like that if you miss out on the first 65 years of life? If we don't take advantage of the time we have right now, we'll miss our kids taking their first steps because mommy had to be at work, or being able to be the first face our kids see when they get home from school.

Time is one of the commodities that we can't get back. So if we can create our own schedule, design our own life around our purpose and reason for being here, then we can enjoy the time we have now and the time we have later. We'll create our own options, and that can include how much time we want to put into our work, when we want to go to the gym, or how much vacation time to take. If you find yourself saying there's not enough time in a day to do the things you love, I hope you realize by reading this book that you can be in charge of your time if you choose.

Financial Freedom

I remember when I was going to college for my undergraduate degree in Communication Disorders and we had to decide if we wanted to take the Speech Pathologist route or the Audiologist route before we graduated. I almost always knew I would choose Audiology. "Just two more years until I have my Masters degree and can start working in the field", I thought. "Not so bad after the four I've already done, I'm more than halfway there!". Until the department dropped a bomb on us. The field of Audiology had decided that they would move from a Masters program to a Doctorate program. Another four years of school. Ouch. They talked it up though, how we would be more respected in the field, be in a better position to find more jobs etc. etc. But no one ever talked about what that meant for our income. No one ever talked about what taking out eight years of school loans would look like, or what jobs would potentially pay an audiologist with their Doctorate degree versus their Masters degree. No one talked about the real world applications of loan repayment, negotiating salary, and retirement options. I feel like they avoided this major conversation about what life would look like when we graduate, and I didn't know enough to ask.

I think in general, school doesn't set us up for success as an adult. Maybe they used to teach how to balance a checkbook, but that's not where we are in 2021. Nobody balances a checkbook anymore. It's not how we live our financial future. We're in this world of bitcoin and investments, and there's not one class in high school or elementary school teaching us how to start investing now. No one talks about how to take a loan out for your house or how to take loans out for school. I mean, we don't really have to wonder why the United States and a lot of the world is in so much debt.

When we come out of school, we have no education on setting ourselves up for financial success.

For most of us, getting 40% of your pay after having worked 40 years is not going to go very far in retirement life. It's going to be pretty difficult to live on. You're going to have to sell some things, maybe get a smaller house or move in with your kids. Remember the time we said we'd get back and all the things we said we'd do "when we retire"? Yeah that's not a reality unless we've set ourselves up financially. The system that we have now doesn't do that. So in order for us to have financial freedom, and in order for us to be successful in our finances, we have to pivot from that old system. We have to start talking more about how that works. For me, it's about being in control of my finances instead of my finances having control over me. How do you achieve this? You design your life on your terms.

It doesn't always look like being your own boss, but if you want more control over your day this is how I get to decide how many hours it takes and what I put into it. If I decide that I would like to make more money because the work that I've created for myself does not take up 40 hours a week, I have the option to create another job for myself where you don't really have that in the typical scenario. I'm free from the restraints that society places on us in a typical job situation. Instead of getting paid per hour, it's now about the value you provide. You're getting rid of the exchange of your time for money when you pivot to your purpose, when you are able to design your life and create your own income. Because I know my worth now, I know what I'm good at, and I know what I'm here and designed to do. I give so much more value in a shorter period of time and I control that financial piece instead of it controlling me.

We Forgot Fun

When adults are asked to rank the key areas of life in order of importance, fun is often last. It's usually what we tell ourselves we 'get to do' if we finish our work. What happens to our lives if we can choose fun instead?

I think that there are people who are really good at having fun and they do it naturally. In fact, there are some people who are way better at having fun than they are at working. And then there are those people who forget that you have to make time to have fun. It's me.

A life without fun is not enjoyable. I had fun as a kid. Everybody has fun as a kid. But when you get so conditioned in trying to meet the expectations of the world, you're on this constant drive to check the box. And checking the box takes a lot of work and a lot of time, and suddenly you're having less fun. They call it "adulting".

I slowly started realizing that there's only one day a week that you actually get to plan for fun. For those of us working a typical Monday through Friday work week, that day is saturday. One whole day away from work, what a privilege! Because Sunday…..Sunday doesn't count. Sometime around 4pm on Sunday you start realizing that you're awfully close to another work day and that rips the fun right out of the day. So what I decided was, I wanted more fun in my life and I realized I had to be the one to create it.

Trust me when I say that once you start to plan fun into your life, you start to realize how good you feel when you have fun every day. And then when you have fun every day, you get more creative. And when you get more creative, you start decreasing your stress levels. And everything gets better when you decrease your stress levels. Your relationships are better, your work is better, your LIFE is ultimately better. And that's what I want for you.

You design your life
on your terms.

Chapter Four

YOUR VIBE ATTRACTS YOUR TRIBE

"Gwen, you seem to be getting younger every year, how is that possible?"

When I look back at pictures even just a few years ago, I can see the loss of direction on my face and just overall "blah" you know what I mean? I can see it in how I held my body, in how I dressed and in my eyes. We think of happiness and satisfaction as feelings but I believe they are just as much a physical and mental state too. So someone who is happier and totally satisfied with the way things

47

are going, looks more vibrant. Someone who doesn't just looks dull. That's hard to explain, but I think you know what I mean. No amount of makeup can cover up what unhappy looks like.

So here's the secret to looking younger and attracting more good into your life - you get back what you put out. Yup, it's that simple.

Has anyone ever told you that you are glowing? I assume you were having a great day that day. Or maybe you've walked into a room where two people had just been fighting and you can somehow feel the negative energy? That's a vibe, or frequency and it can be measured. Sick people emit lower frequencies than healthy people. Happy people emit higher frequencies than sad people. So when you are feeling good in your body, you're radiating high frequencies.

More about exactly HOW to do this later but the point is, if your goal is to attract more good in your life, you have to emit good. If you want to attract more fun, you have to be more fun. If you want to attract more positive people, you have to be more positive. Put out a good vibe and you'll get one in return.

Pivot to Purpose

My first job was in sixth grade, I was twelve. My principal at school allowed me to leave school a little early once a week to walk up the street to my job as a kindergarten cook's assistant. It was the most adorable after school program that taught Kindergarteners how to cook. I imagined having my own kids and teaching them how to cook too. Ever since I was little I dreamt of having kids.

And then when I had my own I could barely get out the door in the morning on time nevermind my dream of leisurely cooked meals and my daughter helping me at the counter. And when I got home from work after, I was the actual Tasmanian Devil

- dinner cooked, child bathed and bedtime all within an hour of being home. And then I collapsed into bed myself. Weekends were spent going out to eat because I just wanted someone to cook for me at that point. There was little room for teaching my daughter how to cook. I was exhausted.

And that's when it really hit me. I dreamt of having kids my whole life and here I was barely able to spend any time with my own. What was the point? I started to worry that her first words would be at daycare and I would miss the only opportunity to hear them for the very first time ever. I feared I wouldn't be able to inspire my daughter because I barely got to see her, that I'd miss out on so much life and time with her and that I'd regret being away from her. I could never get that time back. I realized that something had to change.

When you step back and observe what's going on around you, it's no wonder many women end up stressed out and overwhelmed. It's no wonder we begin feeling hopeless because we're stuck on the hampster wheel of life and have no idea how to get off. Women are frustrated that it's not easy to take time off when they want to. Frustrated that they have to choose work over baseball games and dance recitals. Frustrated that 40 hours a week for 40 years results in 40% of their pay to live on for the rest of their life. The 9-5 hasn't changed since 1920 even though time has drastically changed since then. We might realize we're not living our best life but we don't usually know how to change, so we don't year, after year, after year.

The truth is, we can't turn back the clocks and re-experience a part of our life. We have kids to enjoy them and to love them and to teach them how to be good humans yet we spend less time with our kids than they do with their teachers. How can we be their best example, their best inspiration if we don't get to see them? How can we be their best example if we're living a life that is unfulfilling if all that we wish for our children is that they live out *their* dreams? We can't afford not to pivot and change the way we're living.

Research shows that a lack of mission and achievement is damaging to your health with higher risk of heart disease and stroke. The system is broken. We're churning out stressed out, sleep deprived kids and telling them it's ok because we're doing it too. Something has to change and it has to start with YOU.

About 50% of people dislike their job. And while it makes for great conversation over Friday night drinks, many don't think about the long term health implications job dissatisfaction could be causing.

Jonathan Dirlam, a doctoral student in sociology, set out to investigate the long-term health effects of job satisfaction early on in people's careers.

Together with Hui Zheng, an associate professor of sociology at Ohio State, they set out to analyze date from surveys of 6,432 Americans to analyze their job satisfaction over a number of years starting in 1979. The survey was the National Longitudinal Survey of Youth 1979 (NLSY1979), and the participants were between 14-22 years when the research began.

Participants were asked to rate their job satisfaction level from 1 (dislike very much) to 4 (like very much).

These results were divided into four categories: consistently low job satisfaction (45 percent), consistently high job satisfaction (15 percent), started high but trending down (23 percent), and started low but trending up (17 percent).

Here's the thing, all participants reported some type of health issues after they reached the age of 40. And in case you're like me and wondering how they differentiated health issues as a result of job dissatisfaction and just good old age, the researchers used the consistently high job satisfaction group as a control. Their health problems were compared with the other groups.

Here's what they found. Those who consistently responded in the low satisfaction group reported much higher levels of depression, sleep problems, and excessive worry, and scored lower on mental health measures too.

Those who started off with high job satisfaction, but had a downward trend, were more likely than the consistently satisfied group to report trouble sleeping and excessive worry and had lower mental health scores. However, they did not fair worse on emotional problems.

The group that started with low job satisfaction early on, but trended upward, didn't see extra health problems when compared to the control group.

So when we pull all of that together, it seems that those who fell into the low job satisfaction category were affected more on the mental health front than in physical health. And I'd be willing to bet that this doesn't just apply to someone's career choice. I bet relationships would have similar results.

So if you're like me and you picked a career at eighteen, graduated college, got a job and have been working since, I see you. If you're a mom and your day ends and you probably didn't get to do one single thing you wanted to do for yourself, I see you.

If you keep saying "when my kids grow up I'll _____, or "when I retire I'll finally _____(fill in the blank)." I was you. But what if you don't have to wait? What if you start getting really clear on your values and you begin making sure that your life revolves around them? What happens when instead of putting ourselves last, we put ourselves first and you turn the word selfish into self-seeking. What if this was the solution to finding your life fulfilling purpose and that changed the entire trajectory of your life and the generations to come?

Living longer and healthier lives by living your purpose is much better than living against your purpose by following the checkboxes and seeking approval on everything you do. Choose to change because you know that if you don't you're literally choosing to cut your life short of your full potential.

What if we honored that this pivot could be simple? What if I told you that you were born for greatness with a purpose specific to you and you only and all you needed to do was know how to access it?

Because when we do find our purpose, everything else just makes sense. It allows us to go inward and make that full connection with who we are at the core of everything. I think so often we get caught up in believing that it's individual, that our only goal in life is to show up and be successful for ourselves. But I think that the real truth, and the real reason for having a purpose that is unique to you, is so that you can teach others to do the same. It's all about connectedness with other people, connectedness with the world, and sharing in that community of greatness.

When you're living your purpose, you are happier and more creative. You enjoy the things you do every day, instead of feeling like you have to show up. You create that financial freedom because you learn how to be in control of your finances instead of letting them control you. In fact, you find yourself in the driver's seat of everything you do and therefore have more fun and just live happier and healthier all together.

We have to start thinking and living differently. We have to start teaching differently and it starts with you.

Dreams and Goals

I remember standing in my driveway thinking "Is this it?". I was contemplating my marriage, but leaving felt hard. It was all I had known for nine years. The thought of starting over and having to figure things out on my own is what had stopped me from leaving every time prior. Honestly, I constantly wished he would cheat on me so that I didn't have to be the one to make the choice. I've never said that aloud. But it just felt easier that way. I had thoughts of leaving, but then thought of the money my parents spent on the wedding, and thought of all the family members I had become so close with over the years. I thought of all the things people would say or think about me and I thought about all the people I would let down. And then one day, I got asked a question that changed my entire outlook on life.

I had recently reconnected with a friend of a friend through my work. His band needed musician earplugs so they came in to see me. One day we met for lunch and he just looked at me as if he knew exactly what was going through my head and he said "Gwen, do you love your life, or are you in love with your life?".

Whoa. What scared me most was that I knew the answer immediately, I was NOT in love with my life and for the first time, I realized that I didn't have to stay married just because everyone else expected me to. I was able to step outside the box and remove everyone else's thoughts. The more I thought about it, the more confident I became in myself and listening to what I truly wanted from life.

Before we can decide to change though, we have to get ourselves to recognize that it's even a possibility. I think a lot of people "dream" but they intentionally create this grandiose dream that they believe would only happen if they won the lottery. It's not a dream that they would work towards because they don't truly believe they can make it happen unless it happens by chance.

Have you ever looked at the odds of winning the lottery? Well, according to Insider (magazine?) you're more likely to be killed by hornets, become the President of the United States, or land in the emergency room with a pogo stick related injury than win the lottery. Yes, those are real facts.

When you look at it that way, you can start to see so much missed potential. People are literally sitting on their dream life but thinking the only way out is a lottery ticket. I want you to know that YOU are the lottery ticket.

I could see what my life would look like if I didn't change. I knew I would never be 100% happy, and I knew I would continue to feel unfulfilled. No one wants to have regrets when they're lying on their death bed! I feared one day it would be too late to take any action at all. All I wanted was to be able to write my own rules, to have fun and laugh every day, and for money to flow easily by working a job that I love. I wanted to make a difference in my life and in the lives of others.

When I first started learning how to dream, it all felt impossible. It wasn't like one day I just dreamt of this life I wanted and knew I could design it. I had to hear from people who had gone before me. I had to take my brain to the "gym" and teach it how to flex its muscles. A lot of training had to take place to not only grow muscle but to gain the confidence to flex it….to lead with it. What happens most often is people will state their dream and then automatically decide that it will never happen and they'll never revisit it again. Don't let that be you! We start getting inside of our head and our ego takes over because it wants to protect us. We start to tell ourselves a story that we can't, just because we're not accustomed to dreaming and successfully setting goals to achieve that dream.

We've been primed our whole life to believe that checking the boxes makes you successful. If you graduate high school, then you'll go to college. And if you go to college, then you'll get a job, and your job will be successful, and you'll make enough money, and you'll be able to provide for your family. And after 40 years of work you'll retire and be able to live a cushy life on your pension and retirement. So, to pivot outside of that, the fear that comes up for people when we talk about dreaming your life into existence, is that they'll fail because there's no real checkbox. There's nobody telling them, "Yes, you're right." or "No you're wrong.". Everything is on your shoulders. It's almost like you're jumping off a cliff, hoping that you'll fly and not knowing if you will because you've never been put in that situation before.

There are people who have never dreamt before simply because they don't know they can. I was one of them. These people think that their only choice is to work 40 hours a week, save fun for the weekends, and then retire after 40 years of work. Because it's all we're taught, it's all we see, and it's all we know. Now you know you have options.

People who've done this know that the more we tell our body and our brain what we want, and the more consistent we are in taking action steps to get us closer to that and the more it will become our reality. Dreaming your life into existence is just about getting completely clear on exactly what you want, then telling your brain over and over and over again that it's happening. This is the way that you're going to know that it will be achieved as long as you stick with the process.

I know it sounds crazy. Trust me, the first time someone told me this I didn't believe them either. So I just DREAM my life into existence? Yeah ok.

I just know that I don't want to see my daughter in adrenal fatigue, working a job she hates, just because everyone else is doing it and because the school system teaches us and primes us for factory work. It's not enough to tell our kids they can be whatever they want, because most of the world is not a living example. We can be whatever we want and we can create the life that we want. We don't have to go to school to get a good job. And who gets to decide what a good job is anyway? What if a good job was a job that I decided how much I make and what work I did?

But here's what I now know, you will have a totally different perspective on life after reading this book.

By going through this book, by understanding how to dream, you're going to be able to create a crystal-clear full color dream that only your brain can recognize. If you close your eyes, you will not have a hard time visualizing exactly how you expect your life to look. And then every day little bits and pieces of that dream will become reality because you told it to.

Community and Upskilling

I didn't know I needed community and connection until it literally landed in my lap. Remember how I talked about finding essential oils when my daughter was a newborn? A friend had posted about some products she was using to keep her family healthy. She happened to mention that there was a sale on what she had been using. Now I have FOMO, and when I decide I want something, I just buy it. So I bought the products and before they even showed up at my doorstep I was doing research on how to use them. What I found was a group of women teaching other people how to live a healthier life. I joined the group for education and immediately knew I was supposed to be there.

These women were collaborating, supporting each other, sharing resources and knowledge and what stood out to me the most was that they were earning an income just by helping people find healthier products. These women shared how they were making their own hours, getting healthier themselves and taking charge of their finances. I couldn't believe what I was experiencing. I reached out to my friend who had introduced me to her product and asked her what this was all about.

It wasn't long before I dove in myself. I started participating in personal development, creating a vision board for my desired life and began designing my future.

I don't have to tell you what happens when we don't have community and connection, just look at the year 2020. It's human nature for us to want to belong. We need to feel that connection with people. We need to belong to something almost bigger than ourselves because that's what keeps us going. When we get to do life with others, it motivates us and we get to feel like we're more a part of changing the world for the better than just checking the boxes.

HTTPS://WWW.CDC.GOV/MMWR/VOLUMES/69/WR/ MM6932A1.HTM

In a recent study about mental health in connection to the 2020 pandemic, symptoms of anxiety disorder and depressive disorder were found to have increased considerably in the United States during April–June of 2020, compared with the same period in 2019. Scientific evidence strongly suggests that connection is a core psychological need essential to the feeling of satisfaction with your life.

Brene Brown says "A deep sense of love and belonging is an irresistible need of all people. We are biologically, cognitively, physically, and spiritually wired to love, to be loved, and to belong. When those needs are not met, we don't function as we were meant to."

Mama wasn't wrong when she said you become the average of the five people you spend the most time with. We know that surrounding yourself with positive people creates an even more positive person. We also know that connecting with others gives us more resiliency to bounce back from stressful situations.

Women fear being lonely. We fear being rejected and looking different from other women. Women will say it's hard to make friends, but I just think they're looking in the wrong places. If you're following these tips and getting clear on who you are and what you're meant to do, then you will find your people. All of a sudden they are right in front of you. Trust me! Community isn't really taught in school, and we're certainly not taught to work on self development. We're taught to get good grades (individually) and to meet expectations of teachers and parents - to be approved of, and get a good job. And everything up until that point is individual.

Some people will have a feeling of angst about going from their well-known world to this new world of self-discovery. As you move through this journey of upskilling and self-development, you WILL feel uncertain. You will feel fearful of the changes that you're going through. Part of you is going to push against it. What we're doing is working through dreaming and envisioning how your new life can be. And that's okay. That is part of the transition to anything new. You've already experienced it when you went from junior high to high school, and from high school to college. Every time there is a change and uncertainty, you feel it and you want to push against it. But moving through it has always gotten you to a better location, a better part of your life. This is exactly the same.

The hard part about upskilling is that it sometimes makes you realize that the friends you've been keeping are maybe not your best friends. You start to realize that you want to surround yourself with people who are vibing a little higher. That often means distancing ourselves from the people who have pulled us down. Those are things that we don't realize when we're just going through the routine and doing the same thing every day. All these people may have been pulling you down and not allowing you to become better just by keeping their company. So, a lot of times we find new friends, we find this new community of support, we find people who are doing the things that we want to do and that helps to lift us up through the process. The relationship we have with these new friends is different. It's deeper than the surface relationship that we had with a lot of our older friends. It's supportive. It doesn't take away from our new life like it had been before. There's a sense of belonging by having a community and people that are upskilling and supporting you.

Start becoming aware of the people who are working to level-up their lives. Surround yourself with the people who are already doing it and find influence and inspiration in others who have gone first. Read books and get yourself inside a community so that you can connect with other people who have already been there, and figure out who you want in your life and who you don't want to be spending as much time with.

Opportunity

There is a ladder of learning that exists everywhere in our world, with everything we could possibly learn about. One of the greatest examples I can think about is driving a car. Imagine you have this ladder with four rungs and each rung is a step in learning. The first step is what we call unconscious incompetence. So for example, driving a car, my six year old doesn't really know that she doesn't know how to drive a car. She has absolutely no idea. She is completely unconscious about her incompetence.

The next rung on the ladder is where she realizes, "If I got in that seat to drive the car, I wouldn't actually know how to do it, but I am curious. I want to figure it out. I'm curious about wanting to know how to drive a car." This is the step called consciously incompetent or becoming curious about what she doesn't know.

Step three is taking the steps to begin learning how to do the thing you don't know how to do, driving the car in this instance. But you're still new and still learning. You are at the step of conscious competence.

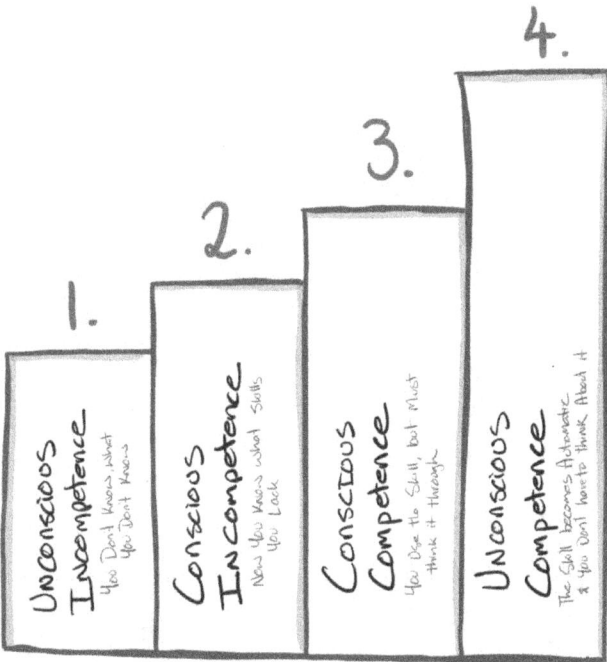

The 4 Stages of Learning

1. Unconscious Incompetence — You Don't Know what You Don't Know

2. Conscious Incompetence — Now You Know what Skills You Lack

3. Conscious Competence — You Use the Skill, but Must think it Through

4. Unconscious Competence — The Skill Becomes Automatic & You Don't have to think About it

When you get to step four, you become unconsciously competent, meaning you could do it in your sleep. You've been driving for years. You can get in any car and know how to drive it. It's so easy for you that you barely have to think about it.

So this ladder makes sense right? You can see how someone starts at the bottom and climbs their way to the top to become competent. But the problem with the ladder of learning is that most people never become curious about what they don't know. Step three and four aren't even a thought because they don't ever get to step two. You've heard people say "you don't know what you don't know", which is true! But if you never get curious, if you don't have your eyes open to look for opportunities, you'll never make it past step one. And what will life look like for you stuck at step one?

Speaking of opportunity, when your eyes are open you know the value of surrounding yourself with the people who have gone before you. If you know to look for opportunity, you can see one in your realm because you've moved up that ladder of learning. You now become curious about how other people have done it and you get yourself involved with this circle of influence, people who are going to help you level-up your life because they have skills that maybe you haven't learned yet, or they've gone before you and you can learn from what they've done.

When we look at our life, especially in the last year with a pandemic that no one was prepared for, we can look back at our past 365 days and decide whether we liked what we saw or we don't. If we don't, then we have the opportunity to decide what we're going to change in order to like the next 365 days and beyond. We have control of that. No one else does. That future hasn't happened and how it happens is what we do moving forward. We can decide to make the next 365 days better.

So how do we change? How do we get to the point of recognizing step two on the ladder and move up? The first step is being aware of your own life, being able to recognize what you love, what you don't love and having the desire to change. It's being open to look for opportunities, it's being aware that maybe there are some parts of life that you don't understand, but you are now curious and open to learning. And when you do that, you open up the rest of those steps on the ladder. You allow yourself to move up and move forward and change the parts of your life that you don't like, moving towards creating a life you truly love.

So the way that we can review the last 365 days of our lives and decide to move ourselves from being consciously unconscious about how we are living our life to being consciously competent, is to be able to reflect on what our life has been like. I want you to spend some time reflecting on these five questions that have been influenced by Tim Ferriss, author of the *4-Hour Workweek* and other books.

The first question is a personal question for me. If you remember, it's the question that allowed me to realize I had been living my life to someone else's standards the whole time. And that question is: Do you love your life or are you in love with your life? And although they sound very similar, they are very, very different. Take time to explore this one in your own life.

The second question is: What would life look like if it were easy? Do you wake up every morning feeling challenged by getting out of bed and heading to your job? Does your day feel stressful and difficult? What does easy look like for your life? How would you visualize how that would look to you? What's involved in that? We assume that our life is a hustle and grind. Society tell us it has to be hard. It has to be a challenge. But it really doesn't have to be. Our life can be something that is easy, that comes naturally, that is purpose-driven. What would your life look like if it was easy? If it was simple? If it was effortless? That's what we're asking.

The third question is: What are the worst things that can happen? If you decide that you're not in love with where you are, what's the worst that can happen if you pivot and make some changes? If you change careers, what's the worst possible scenario that can happen? How bad can it be? How hard would it be to get your job back if you decided to go down a different career path? How hard would it be to leave a marriage and start a new relationship only to realize that maybe the new relationship wasn't exactly what it needed to be for you? What's the worst thing about having the freedom to explore other relationships?

Tim Ferriss talks about an exercise of fear-setting. He talks about how we overestimate how bad things really could be. We overestimate how hard it would be to go back in the steps that we've done. So if you've decided to change your career, we often think that that means that our old career is cut off to us forever. But in reality, it's not. If we sell our house, how hard is it to go back to where we were? And yes, it might cost you time and money, but we want to actually think about what is the worst that can happen? And how bad is that, truthfully?

Often we catastrophize how bad it really is going to be and when we actually put our minds to quantifying what that is, it isn't as bad as the story we created in our minds. And honestly, in our modern society, the worst thing that's going to happen is probably not that bad. You won't give up your job, but you've still got a roof over your head. You've still got a family that lives for you, and you've still got food on the table. You've still got all these things. If you've just lost one part, it's not the end of your life, and you've got the ability to go back and either pick it up or move forward with something else.

Question four is: What's the cost of not pivoting? If you look at your last 365 days, and you don't like what you see but you don't change, what is going to continue to happen? Where will that put you for the rest of your life? What will that mean for you long term? What's the cost of not changing? Will it be a cost to your health, happiness, or relationships?

The last question is something that I ask myself every single day. If you can get in the habit of doing this one every single day, it will bless you. The question is: What can I be grateful for today? So often we get caught up in the hard parts of our day, and we look for people to commiserate with us about the things that were hard instead of reflecting on the things that were great. When we start to do that, we start to increase our frequency, and we increase our vibe, and we create better health and create less stress. So, think of one thing that you can write down that you're grateful for today and if you've got more, keep going!

As creatures that are designed for fight or flight, we look for the warning signs of danger in our life in everything we do. If we only orientate ourselves for the danger in our life, this affects our frequency and what we see or allow into our life. The more bad we look for, the more bad shows up.

So what if we looked for the good every day? If we reset our life to look for what we are grateful for, we start consciously looking for these things. The more you do that, the more you'll actually find things you are grateful for and the happier you'll be. Your body frequency will go higher and higher as you see more and more things to be grateful for every day. They are there, whether you choose to look for them or not. But if you do choose to become aware of the good, you'll attract more and more opportunities and good into your life. Pretty soon the bad things or fears and frustrations that you have, start to disappear and life can look completely different in one years time.

5 questions to ask yourself:

1. Do you love your life or are you in love with your life?

2. What would this look like if it were easy?

3. What are the worst things that could happen?

4. What will life look like if I don't change?

5. What can I be grateful for today?

Chapter Five

WANTING TO BE A DOCTOR

Growing up, I was a competitive gymnast. I spent four hours a night after school in the gym. It was usually 9:30pm by the time I got home. I would sit down, make myself an egg sandwich, and turn on the TV. The only thing that was on at that time was the show, "ER", starring George Clooney. Watching him and connecting with the characters, I could see myself working in the emergency room. I just loved anything surgery. I really thought, "I'm going to be a doctor. That's what I'm going to do."

That was around age 14, right before starting high school. I kept getting little nudges throughout high school to take a different path. My teachers told my parents to set me up with tutoring for the SATs and I remember taking them three times. It was always math that I needed extra help with. It wasn't that anyone actually said, "Hey Gwen, you're not good at math," but I started to observe the way things were happening. My teachers would say, "I will get you into tutoring and you'll do much better." So, as I said, it's not like someone told me specifically that I wasn't good at math, but my grades, the way teachers tried to sway me into different classes, it was apparent what was trying to be conveyed to me.

In high school, I struggled in general, but I struggled in math class specifically. I didn't enjoy it. My guidance counselor told me, "Listen, if you think you're going to be looking at being a doctor, you're going to have to be really proficient in math, and it just doesn't look like that's the way you're headed."

It was then that I said, "Crap. Up until now, I thought I was going to be a doctor. So what do I do? I don't know what other path to take. I'm obviously not smart enough to be a doctor." And that's when I started to look at all that I really knew that seemed feasible for me to be able to succeed at and didn't require much math and that was becoming an artist like my mom.

My mom was a fine artist. She had studied and practiced for years, and taught many classes. She was really good at what she did. I didn't have those same finite skills, so I decided to take a bit of a different route. Since becoming a doctor was out, I decided to pursue art history in college. I nearly failed out my first semester with a 2.3 GPA. It was an eye-opening experience for me. I said, "Alright, I can't fail out of school because I'm not going to get anywhere if I do, so I need to pivot and figure out what I want to do."

That was the first time that I started to explore what my possibilities were. I took a look at the class offerings and landed myself in a class that I really did enjoy. It was about anatomy of the head and the neck. Makes sense that I would love that given my ER obsession. The funny part of the story is, I did end up becoming a doctor but not how I thought I would back when I was watching ER and imagining myself in the emergency room.

These limiting beliefs, the stories that get told to us and things that we embody, make us believe that we can't expand on that knowledge. It leads us to believe we can't grow in that area because someone has told us we didn't have the skillset, so in our minds we think that's the end.

What Made Me Love Math

The core part of my studies in audiology was math so I really did have to know it. If someone asked me to sit down and do calculus on a piece of paper though, I would cringe. The kind of math I was doing was hands on math, it had a purpose and felt relatable. I could connect it with the real world. It was okay because it was leading me to learn more about something that I love. I love learning about the anatomy of the body. I love learning how parts work and I had to use all of that to know how sound comes into the ear, how to measure frequency in cycles per second or hertz.

So all I really needed was relatable material, material that I enjoyed. That's when I could understand math, and that's when I actually started to enjoy it. And now I really love budgeting and doing finances and helping people get on top of their debt. So it's funny how the world can come full circle, but you have to get out of that fixed mindset to allow it to happen.

Fixed vs Growth Mindset

A fixed mindset is something where you believe that the skills that you have are permanent – that there can be no growth in your intelligence and your abilities and that there's no room for change in either direction. A growth mindset is when you believe that you have infinite ability to learn, whatever you want to learn as long as you have the desire to and as long as you put the time into it. A fixed mindset will keep you stuck. You won't be able to see new opportunities in front of you, and you won't be able to advance because you believe that where you are is where you are and it's not going to change.

Growth mindset on the other hand, is taking and growing a mindset anywhere in your life - whatever you're interested in. I never knew about mindset. That word never came up in education. But obviously the story that I was told and believed was that I wasn't good at math. Therefore, I thought, "Well there's a hard stop. I need to do something that math is not involved in because obviously I'm not good at it." That led me into art history, which I quickly realized was not something I was passionate about.

The one thing you need in order to see opportunity and believe you can grow your mind is desire. All you have to have is a desire to learn more, and you will.

Limiting Beliefs

The problem with mindset is that we spend most of our lives taking in information from everybody else. We form our thoughts from the things that surround us such as TV, social media, our teachers, and especially our parents. I think our parents have such good intentions, but they might not realize some of the limiting beliefs that are keeping them small. They might even be carrying forward limiting beliefs that their parents taught them.

I think about how much time as a student you spend with your teachers. It's almost more time than with your parents. So, the people we think are going to be the most influential in what we learn and what we embody, end up maybe not being our parents, but our teachers and the world around us in our social settings.

Trauma and the Great Depression and Limiting Beliefs

Look at trauma, which can be any story in your life. It doesn't have to be physical trauma, it can be emotional trauma or even financial trauma. If we go back to the Great Depression of the 1930s, parents probably talked a lot to their children about what they couldn't afford because they didn't have money to put food on the table and rations were slim, so they were told not to waste any food. This was perfectly acceptable in the 1930's because it was the actual truth. But then, the kids who grew up in that time period embodied the belief that they don't have money and that they couldn't afford to spend outside of the basic necessities. In turn, they told their kids, "We can't afford that." and "Don't waste food," instilling those same beliefs in their kids even if the financial situation in the 1950's looked differently for families than it did in the 1930's. I learned that trauma like that is carried seven generations deep. So, if you could go back even two generations, that's a lot of stories that don't necessarily apply to where we are in the world right now. Whether or not it applies, it's just this belief that we internalize because we've been told it over and over again.

Limiting beliefs are not always financial though. That's just where my brain automatically goes because of my money beliefs. Limiting beliefs can be, "I'm not smart enough." My example of not being great at math, therefore thinking I wasn't smart enough, is a limiting belief. "I don't have enough time," is another one. You could enter basically anything, "I'm not *"blank"* enough. I'm not pretty enough, tall enough, etc." It's just a belief that you embody that stops you from pursuing your best self because you believe that you can't ever get there. You're stuck in this one way of thinking and don't even realize there may be other paths.

So, what do we need to do with our limiting beliefs? We need to rewrite them. First, recognize that they are limiting you, and then learn how to rewrite them so that you can create a future that is something that you truly love, and one that you can be your full, authentic self in.

Eating Disorders and Speaking Kind

What we're told and what is modeled for us is so influential in the way that we think, that really we only need to hear it once for it to affect us forever.

I heard an impactful story about a woman who had suffered for years with an eating disorder. She said that as an early teenager, an uncle had leaned over to her and whispered something in her ear about being a fat kid. This uncle said one thing to her, and that one thing was all it took for this child to begin obsessing over how she looked, which obviously led to obsessing over what she ate. Years of an eating disorder led to many physical and mental issues over one thing that someone said to this girl.

It's so important to remember how powerful our words are. We have to be kind when we're talking to ourselves, talking to kids, remembering that everyone, including ourselves, is so impressionable. This was one of my major reasons for wanting to be home with my kids and ultimately deciding to homeschool them. I knew how much impact other's thoughts and beliefs could have on my children and I wanted to make sure that I gave them the best possible environment to grow their minds in.

Desire and Ladder of Opportunity

I love this quote by Napoleon Hill. "Weak desires bring weak results, just as a small amount of fire brings a small amount of heat." Once I witnessed my own desire to succeed in a field that required math, I desired to choose to live completely differently. I became aware that it was possible. I became obsessed knowing that I *could* live differently, and I became obsessed with figuring out exactly how to do that.

A lot of times, we get stuck on this hamster wheel and we can't figure out how to get off, so we just stay on because it's easier to stay on the wheel than it is to step off and fumble and fail. We've been told over and over again what our life should look like by society's standard, and when we've got a life that looks like "it should" and it's not making us happy, we don't think we have the right to desire anything better or different. We don't believe that we have the ability to grow outside of what society considers to be normal.

It's almost like being on a ladder or a set of stairs and not seeing the next rung or step. So we sit there for a while figuring there's no other place to go. But once you get a glimpse of that next step, you can't not want to climb it, especially if you don't love the step you're on. When you know it exists, you have this desire to step up and check it out, you wanna know exactly what that next step brings. The thing is, everyone desires to be happy. No one desires to be unhappy. But without desire to change, you'll stay in a fixed mindset right where you are. Every choice that we make is usually a choice that is fueled by our desire for happiness.

Lottery

Have you ever woken up and thought, "Okay, today will be better. I can like my job, it does provide for myself and my family. I can do this." and then, you get to the office or log into your computer and it's exactly the same shit on a different day. But tomorrow you'll wake up and do the same thing with the same pep talk met with the same disappointment. At some point you realize that the job you're working is probably not the one you would have chosen if you knew that you could create a job around the life that you desired.

It makes me think about playing the lottery and hoping to be the one out of millions of other people who will win. And you start fantasizing about what you would do, you think, "I'll be able to get out of the rat race." And you don't really care that odds are basically miniscule, you just see this little glimmer of hope without having to do much but buy a ticket. It's the easy way out, the answer to all your problems! You don't have to change your mindset, or change your thinking to get it. It will just land in your lap. Ta Da!

Ironically though, most people who win the lottery claim bankruptcy within three to five years after winning and find themselves back in the same position they were in prior. Why? Because their plan lacked discipline. Winning the lottery didn't require discipline. And if you're not disciplined in general, you're definitely not going to be disciplined with your money, and so you spend it all and go broke.

One fifth of Americans believe that winning the lottery is the most practical way to accumulate a large savings. How likely is it that that's going to happen? Not very. It's the actual desire to change that has to exist in order for us to be disciplined to build and work towards the life that we can be completely and totally be in love with. And most won't do it because they either don't have the examples, or they think it's impossible because their limiting beliefs don't allow them to see the next rung or step ahead. Let this book serve as your example.

Faith

After you have desire, the next step is faith. The definition of faith is having complete trust in someone or something. I think most people associate faith with religion and it can be a part of faith, but it doesn't have to be the only part. I did not grow up very religious so I resonate with a complete trust in the universe. The great thing is, you get to decide who or what you put your faith in. You can have complete trust in God. You can have complete trust in yourself. And you can have complete trust in something that you desire to change.

So, faith is built by a course of action plus emotion. You have to be emotionally attached to the daily steps that you're taking to change your life in order to lead you to the result that you want. I know that you've heard of trusting your gut or following your heart. These are internal signals. Built in faith meters if you will. If there's one thing you take away from this book, I hope it's that you understand every single one of us is born with a purpose and therefore born for greatness. We all have this internal zone of genius and it just has to be turned on. Everything we need to start is built in.

So, when you trust your gut, it's because your gut is literally leading you. It's a physical response, your body is telling you, "Go for it" or "Nope, don't do it". How you feel (like really feel) about the situation is super important. Those are our first signs you can lean into. Being in tune with your body and how your body responds both physically and emotionally, attached to that desire to change, all contributes to being able to have faith to get to where you want to go.

Practice listening to your body. Sometimes it's hard, especially if you didn't grow up that way and you're not used to using those skills. But like anything else, with practice comes proficiency. Learning how to listen to your internal cues will serve you well in your faith. It will be easy for you to make immediate decisions about what feels right and what doesn't.

Here's where you get to pull it all together. If you are unsure about where you are in life and where you want to go. Take a look at the Life by Design framework below. The goal is to align your purpose with a challenging and exciting life. This allows you to create a life and a career that you are in love with. Can you place yourself in a quadrant? It is possible that you've felt hopeless about your current situation or situations in the past. Hopelessness is just where we are out of alignment and we're living a life that is boring or stressful or unfulfilling. If you're living a boring and stressful life that is aligned to your purpose, then your life is unbalanced. And if you're living out of alignment with your purpose but you are living a challenging and exciting life, the likely outcome will be burnout.

When we're able to get our mindset right and we establish that faith, change our beliefs, and have a clear desire for the change that we want to see, we become challenged and excited and aligned to our ultimate purpose. We're no longer in that state of anxiety, burnout, overwhelm, or hopelessness. Here's where you get to live a life by design.

life by Design Matrix

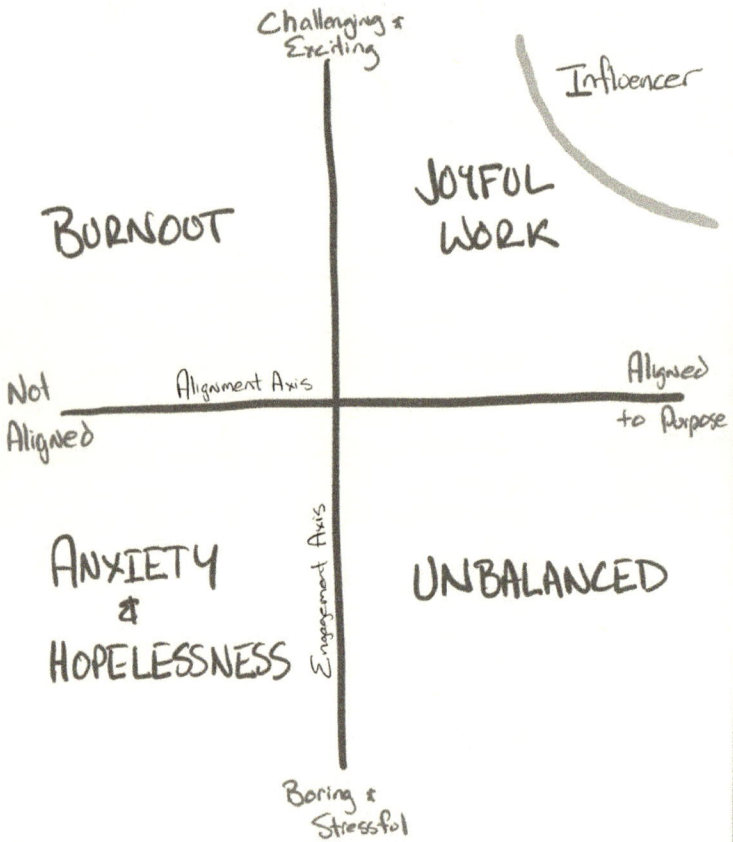

Challenging & Exciting

Influencer

JOYFUL WORK

BURNOUT

Not Aligned — Alignment Axis — Aligned to Purpose

ANXIETY & HOPELESSNESS

Engagement Axis

UNBALANCED

Boring & Stressful

Occasionally I hear a story that makes me think about what's important in my life. Danielle's was just such a story. Danielle is a really, really great friend. She's told this story multiple times and I knew I had to share it with you. It will make you really think about what you value in your life.

I needed one more sign.

I remember asking myself that night, *Am I living in the moment or letting these moments pass me by?* Let me share with you how we went all in on living differently... through a huge PIVOT! I find that everyone usually is waiting for a wake up call: the perfect timing or maybe a sign from God or the Universe to say YES to your Dreams.

In my twenties I traveled the United States, owned hair salons and was very successful behind the chair. I hit age 30 and decided to settle down and have a family. I found the love of my life, named Palmer and had two beautiful children, a girl Preche and a boy Tre. Our life seemed perfect to everyone's eyes, but my husband was a hard working man with a really demanding job on the railroad just like his father-before him. We never saw each other. We didn't get to have a life together. There was no family time. On the inside although things were good we knew there was more! We knew this couldn't be our day-to-day, never seeing each other or our children. Our lives were not balanced at all.

The fall of 2019 I got pregnant with our third child. This pregnancy actually caused my husband to quit his job. He couldn't comprehend not being there anymore for our family. My career as a hairstylist allowed me to replace his income. So we pivoted and went with it.

At that time I was working a ton, even at nine months pregnant. Palmer picked up random jobs on the side just to fill the gaps. But I was now working 50 to 70 hours a week doing hair. I felt like now I was never having time for my family but everyday as I would cry on my way home, I thought this is just a season and we will get through this!

My son Brae was born and I went back to work just 48 hours after he entered this world, never getting to enjoy that newborn time. I can't even imagine doing this again and it kills me to think about that time because I know I can't get it back.

But last year in March 2020 when the Pandemic happened, both our jobs were temporarily on hold. We had no income. Neither of us could go to work. Even with the stress of no income,

I enjoyed those six weeks off. That was like the maternity leave I never got with my newborn but now had with my six month old.

After that we returned back to work and I was now playing catch up on finances and life. I had a taste of family life and balance even during one of the scariest moments in global history.

That August, one night when I got home after work, my kids were in bed and I went to kiss them goodnight. I saw a bunch of checkmarks on the wall next to my daughter's bed. The next morning, I asked Preche what are the checkmarks for. She told me that they were checkmarks for every time that mommy wasn't there to put her to bed. My stomach dropped and I thought the tears driving home where bad… this was like numbness. WHAT am I doing?! I am letting these moments just pass me by!

I already knew things needed to change, but that was the pivotal moment. This is when I wasn't waiting for anymore signs, I was going to design my life how I wanted it to be. I decided then and there I needed to be home to put my kids to bed. I needed a different life. It just was not working for our family anymore. I began working on designing what I wanted it to look like. I began deciding what I needed to change, what I didn't want anymore and how to move forward and change my life for the better.

That fall we decided to sell all material things and start traveling the country as a family and create memories. We said NO to fear and found faith in our new beginnings. We didn't want to raise our kids in fear but up until that point we realized we were barely even raising our children. We have now traveled half the United

States and we share our lives with Living Differently Digitally!

No one wants to be in the space that she was in. But once you get into that space, it's like this realization that, "Oh crap, something needs to change, or this circumstance will never change."

Her story is just one of many friends have shared with me after realizing they were not living the life they truly love.

Values

Values are what you believe are important in life. This is the way you live and the way you work. They are beliefs and principles that actually guide you in the way that you make decisions that affect your everyday life. Your values are connected to your ultimate happiness. So much of our world is connected to tangible things like our home, our car, our clothes, and our toys. You are led to believe that having a lot of things will make you happy. If you look at commercials, the newspaper, and social media with all the ads, it's no wonder that we live in this obsession about buying things to make ourselves look more important.

But the values that I'm talking about are the intangible ones. They're the ones that you cannot touch. Sometimes we can look at the tangible values and peel back the layers to understand why that thing is so valuable to somebody. Like your home. Why do many people value their home? It's a physical thing. But what does it bring you? Does it bring you freedom? Does it bring you fun? Does it bring you creativity? If we look deeper than the surface level, we can usually find out the true intangible values that are housed inside.. Everyone's values will be different.

My values are freedom, authenticity, connection, creativity, security, and honesty. The thing with values is that they can change over time, and they likely WILL change over time. It's great because we experience new things. We climb that ladder of opportunity; we start to experience more of the world and we have a greater vision. Never be afraid to shift your values. So, know ahead of time what your values are, but be open and willing to see what's available to you in the future. That's a great way to look at the way you're living.

If you've never given any thought to values before, you may realize by reading this book that you have taken on someone else's values. When you go through life living for someone else's values, you'll never find balance. You need to go through an exercise which we'll talk about later in this chapter to look at what your values are, not what society tells you your values should be.

Priority

Priority. I know we've all heard this word. It probably comes up in your workplace often. Most of the time, we hear it in a corporate workplace. You sit down in a meeting and the manager says, "Okay, what are the top three priorities today?" And you go through the top three priorities.

But what I learned about the word priority, which completely changed the way I looked at it, was that the original definition was singular. It originated around the 1400s and it meant the state of being earlier, or the first thing to be done. So, you could only have one priority. But after about 1940, the word priority actually became plural. Gone were the days of just ONE important thing, enter the days of juggling multiple priorities at once.

What else happened in the 1940s? World War II ended and we saw more women go into the workforce. We started to see larger families which meant more mouths to feed, and we had all these demands being put on working families. So, it's easy to see how priority changed to priorities. And the funny thing about that is that when that word went from singular to plural, we also saw the words overwhelm and burnout being used more often in society and throughout the world. Raise your hand if you've ever experienced overwhelm and burnout. Sadly, this is really taking a toll on working moms and it's almost become a badge of honor. I don't know about you, but if you've experienced burnout, it's not a good feeling and no one should be honored to be there.

When you're looking at your values, you can have more than one, but what's important is that they all link to the life that you want to live. Everything comes back to that one priority. What do you prioritize in your life? That's a great way to figure out what your values are and what you're working so hard towards. You can't spread yourself too thin in pursuit of your dream life, that defeats the purpose.

One priority at a time.

Yes, you can want to leave your career, start a new career, find the love of your life and travel the world. Those can all be a part of the things that you value. Those are all great dreams and goals. But when you sit down to work on changing your life and rewriting the limiting beliefs holding you back, you have to start with just one. You have to really focus because that's how you become obsessed and that's how you grow your mindset. Prioritizing that one thing is what will fuel you to change your life. And as you begin to change that one priority, watch as the other priorities start to come to life without you even trying.

Alignment to Values

How do you know when you have chosen values that are completely aligned to the life you want to live? You have to ask yourself some questions. When are you the happiest? When do you feel the most fulfilled and satisfied? What do you enjoy doing most? Who do you love spending time with? These are simple questions yes, but they will really give you an idea on what you love doing and where you want to be. You will know your values are aligned to the life you want to live when things feel easy. When there's a flow to life. When you bump into frustration and confusion, that's usually a sign that you're not doing things that are aligned to what you value. Then it's time to re-evaluate.

Your values can also change in priority. One year you might prioritize a value and the next year you might find that it flip flops with something else. Reviewing these things yearly, especially after accomplishing a goal, is pivotal in moving forward and achieving the next goal. You don't achieve a goal and then stop. You say, "Okay, this is great. What did I learn? Where was I the happiest? Where do I feel the most fulfilled? How can I move to that next priority? What's the next thing on the list?" And the best thing about this is, everything you learn moves forward with you. Every step you take is compounding on your last actions.

Downsizing

Sometimes you don't realize you're not living your best life until it gets pointed out to you by someone else. Around the fall of 2017 I read a book called *Disrupt-her* that did exactly what the title suggested. In her book, Miki talks about telling her dad she's pregnant. Her dad asks her when she'll "settle down, buy a house with a yard and a picket fence". She tells him never. She likes her apartment. She likes her community and that they can walk to a playground when they want to. She likes that she borrows what she doesn't have from her neighbors and returns the favor when her neighbors need something she has.

She goes on to talk about how Americans are obsessed with bigger and better things. We buy bigger houses and fill them with stuff. We just keep buying more things. This got me thinking as I lay in my bed, in my very large four bedroom house with a basement full of stuff. I mean "very large" is probably relative, but it was very large for us. I started thinking about all the things we bought and questioned if we truly needed them to live. The more I read, the more aware I had become of how we too had fallen into that trap of living to keep up with everyone else instead of living up to our values. And the more I recognized this, the more I wanted to feel free and think like Miki.

The first time I brought up downsizing to my husband, he was not a fan. But to be honest, he was working a lot and the yard work and housework had fallen on me. I was stressed and overwhelmed just trying to keep up with everything on top of raising two kids at this point. It had been the cause of many fights. And as we started to explore what downsizing could actually look like, we realized that we could move closer to my husband's work and he could come home on his breaks and see the kids. We figured out we would save a ton of money, and my husband wouldn't have to work as much which meant more family dinners and more spontaneous road trips. We we're starting to thin out our life and get clear on wants versus needs.

Eventually, we decided to pull the trigger, sell our house and move into a condo. Man, there's nothing like losing 1,200 square feet of living space and giving up a basement to help you realize what things you really need, and what things you can live without. By doing this though we were able to get really clear on what we valued in life. Spending time with each other and with our family, working less, having more fun, saving more money, going on more trips and creating more experiences were all high on our list.

And then the pandemic of 2020 happened, and we re-evaluated our values again. I think a lot of people did in 2020. We realized that we valued privacy and land that we could sustain our family on someday. So we up and moved again. I don't recommend moving two times in two years, but I do recommend re-visiting your values annually and even more importantly, re-visiting your individual values as well as your family values because they can be different.

How Values Help You Make Choices

How do values help you make choices? When you know your own values, you can use them to help make decisions about how to live and how to design your life. If you know, for example, that you value family and connection time, it's likely that working 70- or 80-hour workweeks is not going to satisfy the value of family and connection no matter how much money you make. So the truth is, that life is actually easier when you live up to your values. I think that that's something that isn't talked about. Even in high school, when we're looking at moving on to college, no one talks about what we value. Instead, it's all about, "What do you want to be when you grow up?" or "What kind of job do you want?" without helping students dive into the why.

The kicker is, value-based choices are not always the easiest choices to make. So, because it's hard and requires more discipline, it's a choice that doesn't often get made. We know what happens when we don't live up to our values. We know that we end up in overwhelm, stress and burnout, and working jobs that we don't love. We lose sight of our true happiness.

What I want you to do now is think about what your values are. In the table below, list your values. You're going to be listing anywhere from three to ten. Don't list any more than 10 because then you are spreading yourself too thin. To help you get through this, let me talk you through some examples of how to think of what a value is.

Previously, I listed off a couple of my values, freedom, authenticity, connection, creativity, honesty and fun. And I know that sometimes it's hard to sit and think about what you value if you've never had to answer this question before. Here's where the internet is extremely helpful. You can literally look up a list of values. Don't go through that list and just pick ones and put them on the table. The point of writing this list is to write down the ones that really mean something to you. Sit with the words you're reading and see if they connect with who you are and who you want to be. You should feel a flutter in your heart or stomach when someone says one of your values. You should feel connected to that value. That's how you know you're on the right track.

My Values

- [ ] _____
- [ ] _____
- [ ] _____
- [ ] _____
- [ ] _____
- [ ] _____
- [ ] _____
- [ ] _____

After you've listed your values, put the list aside, and then come back to them hours or days later. Rewrite it out again to see whether or not your mind has changed. Do this over time to make sure that your body and your heart are aligning your mind with your values.

Chapter Six

SELF-CARE

Pinkeye and Adrenal Fatigue

I had been working as a Doctor of Audiology for about eight years. I had switched jobs three times and each time I switched, I had high hopes that this time would be different. The next setting would be the one that I would actually love. And yet I found myself for the third time, in a job that I didn't love. There was a lot of stress at work. I never knew what mood my boss would be in, I was feeling stressed and under pressure with being on time each day for daycare drop-off, remembering to pack everything the kids needed, packing my own lunch, and desperately trying to keep myself healthy and calm for my family. I'm sure you can relate, there were many moving parts. And everything came home with me from work, which meant that I exuded my stress on everyone in my household.

My relationship with my husband was trying. We never got in bed at the same time because he had to wake up early for work and I had to finish putting everything away from the day only to do it again the next day. There was a lot of resentment. I should have been asking for help and I wasn't because I just didn't know how. I don't know about you but, I thought my husband just knew what was going on and what needed to be done. I thought he was a mind reader, and obviously he's not. Nobody is. The stress just kept piling up to a point where everything, even the smallest little thing, would set us off. We didn't have a bad relationship, but there were some hard days with a newborn baby at home.

Both of us were working and trying to just keep up. That's when my daughter got conjunctivitis at daycare, or as it's lovingly called "pink eye". I was no stranger to pink eye. I got it a ton as a kid. Did you know breastmilk is the best thing ever for pink eye? Worked like a charm for my daughter! I thought I had escaped it, but lo and behold I too caught pink eye. But this time it was different. It lingered and even with a prescription it just would not go away. I've never had anything like this in my life. I'm usually really in tune with my body. I know when I'm healthy, I know when I'm not healthy. And when I'm not healthy I've got all the tricks. I kid you not, I tried everything to heal this pink eye but it never went away. I just knew at that point something more was going on, something other than just this physical ailment on the outside.

So, I ended up in my naturopath's office because I couldn't figure it out. She said, "Yeah, you've got a good case of conjunctivitis but you're also on the verge of adrenal fatigue." But you, as a reader, probably already figured that out, right? I just talked about all the stress in my life, and how I just kept burying it thinking that it would change at some point, but it didn't. I internalized it inside my body, and it came out physically. So, it wasn't really just pink eye. My physical body was telling me at that point, "Warning! You're on overload. You need to stop. You're about to burn out." But did I listen? Not then.

The thing that I tell people is, it was so easy to get there. It was so easy to get ill, but it was so hard to climb back out of adrenal fatigue and change in order to avoid that same situation again. One of the hardest things I remember about that time was that I just didn't feel like myself. I couldn't be creative because this physical and mental ailment was weighing me down. I had poor relationship skills with my husband, the person who's supposed to be my partner and better half. It just felt like I was pouring from an empty cup every single day.

It's not something that just happens overnight. It's something that creeps in day in and day out as we go on the hamster wheel of what a "normal life" is supposed to look like. And we don't just go from healthy to adrenal fatigue. It is a gradual, slow process that you yourself don't always see happening if you're not keen to looking. I remember my naturopath asking me before the diagnosis, "Are you stressed?" and do you know what I said? "Not really." Ha! Obviously, I was.

I learned many things that day. The first thing I learned was that I was making my stress worse by pushing my body to the limits in my workouts. I also learned that communication is very, very important. And most importantly, I learned that regular self-care is absolutely necessary. Because I hadn't been doing that, I had to carve out time for extreme healing. Four hours a week I was in my naturopath's office for sauna, foot bath and colonic treatments. I also had to change my diet and bring in more foods that supported my nutritional needs. I made it a point to get in bed with my husband at least once a week regardless of what else needed to be done before bed. And I started to incorporate more yoga and cut back on the extreme exercise.

The Frog Fable

It reminds me of the fable about the frog and boiling water. If you take a frog and drop it into boiling water, the frog knows that it's dangerous because it's hot, so he jumps out. But if you take that frog and put it in cold water, and slowly bring it to a boil, he doesn't recognize that the water is heating up around him until it's too late. Living a life that is not our ideal life is like being that frog in the water. We don't realize that our bodies are taking on stress until we hit a wall, or in my case, adrenal fatigue.

Self-Care

So, what is self-care? This is one of my favorite topics to talk about because there's this misconception with self-care where everybody thinks that it means that it's only for women when it's not. They also think it means going to a spa, for example. And while that definitely can be self-care, that's not all it is. Self-care is really just taking care of yourself. Sounds easy right? But as moms, all of our care usually goes to our kids and then our job, and then our home and somehow we've landed last on the list, too tired at the end of the day to do anything about it.

Once I became aware I started to look around me and see where the hang up was. I thought back to being pregnant because when you're pregnant you do everything possible to keep that baby healthy. You eat all these really great foods, you make sure that you're not consuming toxic products, you integrate exercise daily, you play nice music for the baby, and you read to it. Then the baby's born and you stop doing all of those things for yourself when in reality, you were growing a human in your body so that's what made you think, "Well, I have to nourish this human. I have to really help it grow and care for it and make sure that it has the best of the best." But what I want to know is, after you have the baby, what happens to the human who carried it?

You yourself are growing every single day. So why do we stop reading? Why do we stop talking nicely to ourselves and exercising and nourishing our body with good foods? Self-care is the easiest thing, but also the hardest thing because we completely lose the thought that we are a growing human ourselves.

Self-care is recognizing your worth. It is knowing that you deserve time for yourself. It's all about things that you love, and the things that light you up. It can take five or ten minutes in your day and can look like reading, walking, listening to music, going out in nature, grounding, or learning about things that interest you. Sleep is one of the most pivotal self-care things you can do, and everyone can sleep! That's the thing about self-care, every single person can perform self-care. But somehow, we let that slip away.

So why am I even talking about self-care? It replenishes us and you feel great, but it's deeper than that. Self-care reduces stress. If there's anything I've learned from my own adrenal fatigue story, it is that stress just sneaks up on you fast and it accumulates in the body over time. So, taking care of yourself along the way allows you to be a better communicator with yourself because you'll understand your body and your feelings. You'll become more in tune with what you need, when you need it. It also makes you a better communicator with the people in your life too. By partaking you become a better partner, a better parent, your immune system is stronger, you feel good about yourself, and you have balance and purpose in your life. And that alone is worth all the self-care in the world.

Implementing Self-Care

If there's one message I'm sending you in this book, it's that implementing self-care does not look like a spa date once a year. I'm going to teach you how to easily implement self-care daily so that it becomes a consistent habit. But you do have to get clear on what self-care means to you, and sometimes you do have to schedule it in. There are days when we have a lot of things going on and a small amount of time. If you don't actively put that on your calendar, you'll skip it because you'll be too tired at the end of the night.

For example, I schedule 10 minutes a day for reading in my calendar and working out before 7:30 in the morning. If I don't schedule it and put it on my daily action steps, I am more likely to press snooze on my alarm clock and not read or workout. And then by the end of the night, I'm too tired to open my book and read consistently. So being consistent with your self-care is not always the same thing every day, but consistently showing up for yourself will make a huge difference.

I was reading a book by Tim Ferriss called *Tools of Titans*. He interviewed billionaires, icons, and world class performers and then wrote about the tactics, routines and habits of each one. He said more than 80% of these people that he interviewed had some sort of daily mindfulness or meditation practice. Meditation scares people, but it doesn't have to be anything that is concrete. It's literally just sitting with your own thoughts for five minutes a day. So even if you think you don't know how, and you think you don't know what you're doing, you can start doing self-care today.

If you have children or you live with someone, it's also important to tell them that you'll be prioritizing self-care so they can respect your time. If they know you take 10 minutes every morning, they know to give you your time.

Before I go to bed, I like to clean the kitchen so that when I get up in the morning, everything's ready to go. My husband, on the other hand, could care less about cleaning up the kitchen. He'll do it whenever he feels like it. When he's done for the day, then he's done. That's where this lack of communication between partners can form resentment because he prioritizes bed time by a specific time and I prioritize cleaning the kitchen before bed. All we have to do is say, "Listen, I prioritize cleaning the kitchen. If you're around and you are not too tired and you would like to assist me, that would be great. If you are done for the day and you prioritize going to bed, then I am okay with you going to bed." There just needs to be that communication. He needs to say, "Hey, I'm done for the day. I can't do anymore. I'm going to go to bed." And now you've talked about it. Sometimes the priorities don't align and you expect the other person to do something, but you haven't actually talked about it. Remember that communication is key.

Another pillar of self-care that everyone can do is prioritizing your sleep, diet, and hydration. These are the three best things that you can do for yourself, and you can do them every single day without really carving out extra time in the day. These things will fix 85% of your life if you prioritize them in your life every single day.

Why is Self-Care Important?

So you already know that self-care is important because it makes you feel good and it decreases stress, but did you know that practicing self-care improves your self-esteem? It improves the way we think about ourselves as being worthy of receiving love, care, affection, and abundance, not just financially, but abundance in all areas of life. We miss this step. So often self-care gets written off. You think, "Ah, I'll do that another day." But, you cannot move forward in life until you think that you are worthy of receiving whatever it is that you wish to receive - your values, your freedom, your connection, your family time. If you don't care for yourself first, you'll never find yourself worthy enough to create that life that you ultimately desire.

There are so many people in this world who have crippling anxiety and depression, people with mental health difficulties. Our doctors are overwhelmed. More often than not, you get a 15 minute appointment and your doctor runs five minutes late, and now your appointment is 10 minutes long. He or she sits down and says, "Okay, you're anxious. You're going to take this medicine and you're going to be fine." No one is talking about what can be done to improve ourselves from the inside out. If we did, that would improve everyone's life tenfold.

Start Small

So, if you're not convinced yet that you need self-care in your life, let's look at a trial run. Decide what one piece of self-care can look like for you and then commit to doing that one thing daily for 5 minutes a day. Start small and read a book for 5 minutes. And then as you get used to that habit, extend that to include other things, until you get to a point where you know that you're fully recharging your batteries every day. But start small, and then build from there

5 Pillars of Self-Care

These are the five pillars of self-care:

1. Emotional wellness + connection - getting clear on who you are and understanding your emotions. Connecting with others who you like spending time with and actually spending time with them.

2. Grounding - with the energy of the earth. Rooting down in order to rise up. Bare feet on the ground, yoga, diffusing essential oils to balance your frequency.

3. Physical health – exercise, diet and water, sleep.

4. Personal development - grow your mind by taking part in things you like to learn about. Read, listen to podcasts, attend trainings, workshops.

5. Fun - can you put a definition to fun? One of my daily action steps is to smile every day. What does fun look like for you? How can you have a little bit of laughter at the dinner table or before bed with the kids. Where can you sneak fun into your day?

Your self-care routine should include something from all of these pillars. If you're not doing any self-care at the moment, just pick one.

One of the best things I ever started doing was the Five-Minute Journal. You do it in two parts - before you go to bed at night and when you wake up in the morning. It literally takes no more than five minutes a day. You write three things down that you're grateful for, three things that you wish to happen that day, and three things that you would change. At the end of the night, you can look at what you wrote in the morning and reflect on your day.

Chapter Seven

LIVING THE DREAM

The Text that Changed Everything

I finally got fed up with our debt and decided that I wanted to learn how to be financially independent. After becoming a certified financial coach, I knew the first thing that needed to happen was that we needed to pay down some debt. And as I started attacking my debt, paying down $25,000 in 5 months, I started sharing what I was doing and helping others in their debt payoff journey too. My friend texted me one day and told me that her and her husband got rid of their "super expensive cars" and they were now on a faster path to becoming debt free. Obviously I jumped with joy! I was elated they were feeling lighter both physically and mentally by making that big financial decision.

But what she shared next was the most pivotal for me. She said "It's just knowing we DO have the power to make life the way we want it and don't HAVE to follow society and what society says is the American dream."

This.

These expectations that live among us are always being pushed on us but no one really talks about them. We are expected to go to school, find a "good job", buy a house, have a family and all the while everyone's trying to keep up with the Joneses. Loan companies make it easy to max out on the nicest cars and biggest houses, and credit card companies fill up the mailbox with offers for more credit. Until one day we find ourselves living this life that we don't love, wondering how we got there.

School System

The question that comes up in my mind is, "Why didn't anyone teach me that I was supposed to dream for myself and not try to live up to everybody else's dreams?" When I think about that, and I look back, I can see exactly where it went wrong. If we look at how our school systems are run, we see that we study the material, we take the test, and we either pass or we fail. We spend 13 years of school and then more if you go on to college, just seeking the approval of other people. So it makes sense that when we enter the workforce, we continue in that pattern. And honestly, because we've been so programmed to meet society's expectations, it's no wonder it continues into adulthood – first marriage, then kids and buying a home. We just get so caught up in other people's expectations of us, that we haven't had a second to stop and think about what we expect of ourselves. And that's exactly how my dreams began - by letting go of the expectation of society, and starting to create my own life, realizing that I didn't have to do what everyone else was doing and that it was ok to create something different.

And if you look around, you can see how this is reflected not just in our school system, but also in the entertainment we watch, the books we read and the movies we see. They all take us through a set way of how our life should look, setting the expectations in our heads of what society expects us to do.

Fixed Mindset vs Growth Mindset

The old way of meeting certain expectations led us to believe that failing meant you were not smart. If you fail, you're not worthy. If you fail, you're a failure. In the new way of thinking, the one I'm proposing you adapt here in this book, we can look at failure as a pivot. As learning and experimenting to find what lights us up. What if we looked at failure as a way to show up 100% authentically?

The new system is about a growth mindset, where failure is no reflection on us. It is just a reflection on what we tried that didn't work. Imagine what we as a society could learn by reframing failure in that way? I challenge you to try it.

If you look at the most interesting people who live the life that you wish you could live, and you talk to them about their life, you will hear multiple stories of failure and what they've learned from it. If you talk to somebody who hasn't changed or is fixed on living up to society's expectations, you will not hear them talk about any failures because they didn't stretch themselves enough to fail. They got comfortable with not rocking the boat. It's likely they don't live the life they truly desire, and it's also likely that they aren't aware they can.

Startup Business Tips

Tim Ferris talks a lot about startup businesses because he's contributed to many and seen great financial success. One of the tips he has about investing in a startup business is to ask the owner of the startup if they've started other businesses before. If they have, Ferris recommends asking them if they've done any that have failed. If they answer yes, it will prove that they figured it out. They pivoted, they shifted and they moved on. What he says is that when you're looking at investing with someone who's starting a business, it's actually extremely important that they have tried and failed before and learned to let go of that failure knowing failure doesn't define their future. That's what I want every human to understand and embrace.

7 Key Areas by the Oola Guys

If you've been living up to somebody else's expectations for a while, it's not always easy to start fresh. But there are some baby steps people can make in order to begin letting go of old expectations. One way to start is with self-love and self-worth which you're already doing, because you read the last chapter.

But from there, you've got to figure out where in the seven key areas of life you're not completely happy. The seven key areas are something that I learned from Dr. Dave Braun and Dr. Troy Amdahl, also known as the "Oola Guys". They say that your whole life can be broken down into seven key areas:

7 key Areas of life according to the Oola guys

1. Faith - complete trust in someone or something

2. Family - the people you live with whether related or not

3. Fitness - exercise and your health

4. Fun - enjoyment in life

5. Field - your career

6. Finances - your wealth, achieving the level that you want to achieve

7. Friends - your inner circle, your acquaintances; the people you choose to spend your time with

OOLA Wheel

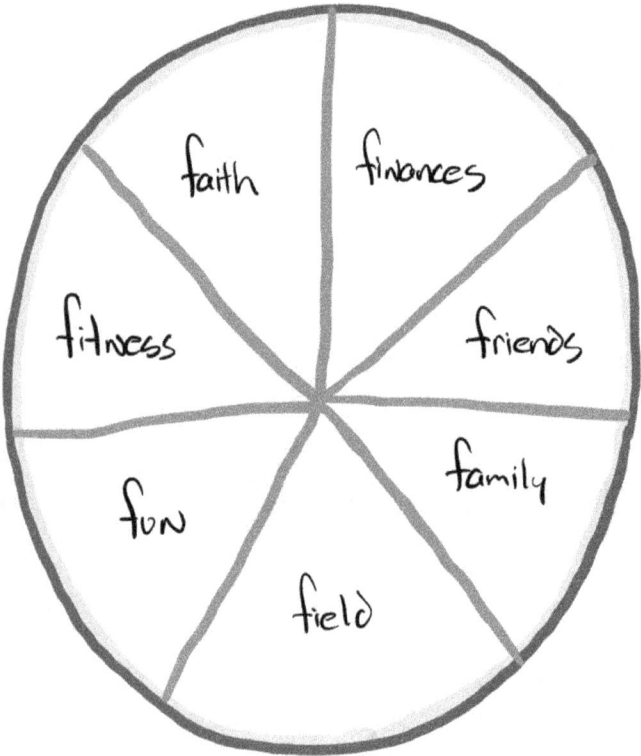

Looking at each one separately, ask yourself:

1. Am I happy in each category?

2. Which one brings me the most stress?

3. Which one brings me the most overwhelm?

4. Which areas bring me the most happiness?

5. Which ones bring me the least happiness?

6. Am I living for myself in this area of life?

7. Am I living for someone else's dreams?

8. Am I working at a job that I don't love and if so, is it possible it's because it's not aligned with my mission and my dream yet?

9. Am I working at a job where I'm not in alignment with the owner's dream or purpose?

(Maybe you're working in a job and you're helping someone else build their dream instead of you building yours. If you don't work to build your dream, someone else will hire you to help build theirs. You can ask me how I know that - because I've been there).

Getting clear on the key areas will take some time and probably some experimenting. Things you thought were really clear to you before may seem not as clear now. Take some time to answer these questions and keep them in the forefront of your mind as you go throughout your days.

Chapter Eight

QUITTING MY JOB

The Four-Year Career

Let's go back to when I returned to work after I had been out on maternity leave and my boss decreased my salary by $15,000. I was stuck between a rock and a hard place. I had to go back to work. We had created our life based on what my income looked like and what my husband's income looked like before the $15,000 reduction. My current pay wasn't going to leave us much wiggle room, so I knew I had to pivot and do something about it.

I read a book called *The Four-Year Career* and it opened my eyes to the possibility of being able to create a job that I loved, create an income that could support us, and eventually leave my office job so that I could have that freedom of time that I valued so much. So, once I read that book and I heard from other people who were doing it, I became part of a community where other women were working towards the same goal, where they were pursuing personal development, and talking about finances and all the other things that had never been brought to my attention.

I said to myself, "Listen, in four years or less, I'm going to leave my office job, and this side hustle that I started will become my full-time gig. It will provide for my family monetarily and I will be able to work from home." That set me on the path of setting my first goal and living out my first dream of being able to create my own time and design my own life.

In 2018, three years after I read the book, I finally got the courage to complete that goal. I sat down in my boss's office and told him that I was giving my 30-day notice. I remember exactly how that felt sitting in that office. I could feel the emotion rising up in my chest. My throat got tight and I knew I could cry at any moment. I wasn't crying because it was upsetting; I was crying because I finally had the freedom to do this. It was so freeing for me to be able to go in there and let him know I had made this decision. I knew I was free to go and create the life that I really wanted to live, and stop working at a job that didn't bring me joy and didn't allow me to live my purpose.

The Scene from The Notebook

In the movie, *The Notebook*, there's a scene when Rachel McAdams is about to leave Ryan Gosling after several amazing days together. She decides that she needs to go back to her fiance'. Ryan wants her to stay so he says to her, "Stop thinking about what I want, and what he wants, and what your parents want. What do you want?" Rachel's response to him is, "It's not that simple." She says she has to go back because she knows what expectations her family has as far as who she should marry, what job her husband should have, and how much money they should make. Ryan Gosling didn't fit that bill for her family and Rachel battles listening to her heart or meeting her family's expectations.

If you don't know that scene, I highly suggest you watch it because there's this internal battle that's happening in her body, where she's afraid to go with her gut and her heart. She's feeling stuck with the decision that she knows will make her parents happy, but ultimately won't make her happy in the end. The funny thing about her response of, "It's not that simple," is that it actually IS simple.

It would be simple if you've been following the path that we've been talking about in this book, in answering the question about what we really want, and so at some point, we must get super clear on what makes us happy. The good news is that all the work that you've done up until now is helping you get there with your values and your mindset and your rewritten beliefs and your new self-care practices. You're more aware now on how to get really clear on who you really are and what you truly want out of life.

Drawing a Picture About Your Life

There is a really simple way to figure out what you love about your life, what you don't love about it, and where you want it to go. All you need to do is draw a picture. Put a line at the top of the paper from the left to the right, and then a line straight down the middle from the top to the bottom. On the left, you simply write, "Don't like". And on the right you write, "Do like". On the left, draw what your life looks like right now in black and white with a pen or pencil. Draw what you don't like about what's going on in your life right now where you are.

If you're not an artist, it doesn't matter. They can be stick figures, it can be a work of art, it can be anything in between. It's not about the art, it's about the image.

Now you get to use all your markers, crayons and colored pencils and on the right side of the paper, draw the life that you dream of having. This is where you get really clear on what it is that you want to see differently. What things will make your life easy and fun?

5 Questions to change your life

Answer the five questions we talked about earlier in the book. They are:

1. Do you love your life? Or are you in love with your life?

2. What would this look like if it were easy?

3. What are the worst things that could happen?

4. What will life look like if you don't change?

5. What can you be grateful for today?

Back in 2016, I was one year into my personal development journey. I already knew at that point things needed to change. I was starting to develop my mindset more and I was really working on ME. I'll never forget it. I knew so clearly what I didn't love about the life that I was currently living. It was so easy for me to draw that black and white picture on the left hand side. I drew an empty bank account, a ball and chain on my leg, and a clock with a big X through it. I can still see it perfectly in my mind.

On the right side of the paper I drew a world with people standing all around it, hands clasped together, I drew a clock, big bright and beautiful, I drew money in the bank, and big muscles on my arms.

And then this past year, I joined the Oola team and I became a certified Oola coach and financial coach because I knew that I wanted to fix my finances and I knew that I was good at helping people find their purpose and live out their dreams. Oola aligns perfectly with that.

What happened next is that they launched this fully digital framework that allows people to basically have a life coach in their pocket. It's a personalized program that learns you as you go and helps you achieve your dreams and goals. They released a short, animated product video and when this video rolled out, I think I watched it with my mouth wide open because all of the images used in the animation were the images that I had drawn on the right-hand side of the paper in 2016.

In 2016 when I drew on the left-hand side, I didn't like that I was living paycheck to paycheck. I didn't like that I didn't have time to work out. There wasn't any time to spend with family. And when this video was released, all the pictures were of the things that I envisioned changing. I envisioned getting up and working out on my time and there was an image of a woman lifting weights. I mean, everything that was in this commercial was exactly what I had drawn on the right-hand side of the paper. It was like they had tapped into my brain to create this commercial.

With the picture, we're literally creating our dream life. And that's how powerful this activity is - the power to create it is in your hands with pen and paper first. Because if you can't see where you're going, you'll never get there. And I may not have known exactly how I would create the picture on the right but trusting myself has been the guiding light. What you would love to see happen in your life in the future. What do you dream of being so very different from here?

Goals and Dreams

Most people think that dreams are something you create in your mind, taking any shape or form, while goals are based on physically taking action on something. What I believe is that dreams are what we're going for and goals are what help us to get there. So both dreams and goals require focus, attention and consistency. You've probably set goals before in your life. But did you set good goals? How do you know? Goals need to be really detailed and specific, and they need to have time attached to them.

For example, that picture that you just drew of our dream life - when I drew myself working out in the morning, or on my own time, that was my dream. That's what I wanted my life to look like. But the goal for me to get there was a certain income monthly that would allow me to quit my office job and work from home.

And that goal of making a specific income would be broken down into specific steps that would get me there like working an hour a day on my business, helping a certain amount of people to get to my goal, and setting time specific completion dates.

The goals need to be really specific and have details and a time attached to them because, for instance, if you set a goal to "get a good job", that could mean anything. It's not specific enough for your brain to know exactly how to achieve that goal. The brain needs to know what a good job is, and it needs to see and hear it over and over again until it believes it to be true. What if you change the goal "get a good job" to "working my dream job at such and such a place by December 2022"? You now gave your brain and your body very specific information. And continually accessing that goal, reading it daily when you brush your teeth or seeing it in picture form allows your brain to embody that achievement. The more that you tell it that and the more that you work towards those things, the faster that goal will become truth.

If we remember that goals are what we achieve in order for us to live our dream life, and that our dream life should be the most vivid, colorful picture that we can possibly create in our mind, then we should be able to state our goal and feel in our body what achieving that goal will do for us, our family and our future.

When I work with clients helping them set their goals or imagine their dream life, I have them close their eyes and think about what it would feel like to be there. I ask them to imagine their favorite color coming in through the top of their head and drowning their whole body in color. Down through the arms, the belly, the legs and out the feet. I ask them to pay attention to temperature and what they feel in their whole body in that moment. Usually it evokes a smile, and sometimes tears of happiness because they can see and feel so clearly that dream life coming true.

Do me a favor and close your eyes. Envision your color entering your head and filling up all the spaces inside your body. Get quiet and feel the emotions attached to it. What does it feel like for you? What do you see? How happy are you? Do this as often as you can because as soon as you can attach emotion to your goals, it will connect you to the desire to begin and ultimately lead you to your dream life.

If you take small daily actions, it will lead to big results. Just three daily steps towards your goal are over 1,000 steps per year. That's impactful! One thing to remember when setting your goals is that we often overestimate what we can do in a day, and we underestimate what we can do in a year. Getting clear on the three action steps a day will help you set achievable short term and long term goals. It will also allow for quick wins and a chance for your brain and body to get used to making progress and achieving a goal. When we overestimate what we can do in a day, and we end up "failing" because we didn't do it all, it's harder to keep our brain and body aligned to the big goal. But if we can create quick wins by staying realistic with our goals, we'll have the motivation to keep going.

For example, I have a goal of paying down debt. I started with the smallest debt first, which I knew should take no more than 30 days to achieve. And by starting with the smallest debt first, I was able to experience a quick win when I paid it off in the 30 days. This gave my brain and body a jolt of excitement and feelings of accomplishment. These are just little tricks that help keep us moving towards bigger goals. Paying down my debt might seem like a really big goal overall, but if I can start by paying down one debt, and hit a mini-goal on the way, it allows my body to get used to winning and get used to pushing more. This creates consistency and new habits you're more likely to stick to. Showing up with your daily actions to achieve little tiny goals along the way will lead to accomplishing your big goal in the end. If we start out with too big of a goal, it will take you too long to get to the reward which will make you less likely to keep going.

Accountability

Now you know you've got to take action steps every day and be consistent to create new habits. But it's almost not enough for us to do it alone. And this is what allowed me to see the power of community way back in 2015. I stepped my feet into that community without knowing what it was going to do for me, and it actually ended up being a huge support system. It ended up being a place where I could learn from other people and we could cheer each other on. Community is what made me see my goals were possible.

If you've ever ridden on a Peloton bike before or had the Peloton app, you know what having a community looks like going alongside you as you're biking. People are high-fiving you and you can high-five them back and you can see where you are on the leaderboard. You can connect with your friends across the country and hop on a ride "together". It's that community that keeps people coming back to Peloton. It's fun. There is a sense of camaraderie because they know that there are other people doing it with them. I can only imagine if you just saw your instructor on the screen and you couldn't see if anybody else was doing the same ride. It would be so much harder to get up and get on that bike if you didn't know that there are other people who are working towards a similar goal.

Accountability will only boost your confidence and accelerate your success. Here are three ways to help you be accountable:

1. Join my free Facebook group. http://www.inspiredandready.com Me and other people in the community share tips, tricks and accountability on how to move forward in your journey to get to your dream life.

2. Get together with a group of friends, read this book, work through the exercises in this book together, and meet regularly to hold each other accountable to the dream life and the goals that you've set for yourself.

3. Find a mentor or coach who has already travelled this path before you who can hold you accountable and give you guidance along the path.

Power of Visualization

Friday afternoon, the day before the big gymnastics meets, all the gymnasts would sit on the floor together. Everyone's eyes would be closed and there would be complete silence. We would sit there and visualize each of our routines on every single piece of equipment until that routine was absolutely perfect. If you were visualizing yourself performing your routine on the beam and you fell off, you would start at the very beginning again until you have visualized a perfect routine. Once you've perfected the beam routine, you could move on to the bars, the floor, and the vault. And you would start that process over again for each new piece of equipment, visualizing your routine until every single move is absolutely perfect, there are no falls and you get a perfect score.

What I didn't know at the time, was that my coach was teaching us the power of visualization. First he would gather us around the TV and have us watch one of the scenes in Rocky, the movie. And at the time, I was young. I mean, I had no idea what visualization was. And we always laughed and poked fun at the fact that he made us watch Rocky. We didn't understand it. But what he was teaching us is that the power of visualization will get you exactly where you want to go because you are teaching your brain exactly what you expect your body to do.

Visualization is really just a picture of the things that you desire in life that you see when you close your eyes. So look at that picture that you just drew of the dream life on the right-hand side of your paper. When you close your eyes, you should be able to see exactly what your life looks like running through each of those elements that are part of your dream life. Not only is it a picture, but it's also a feeling inside your body. It's attached to that emotion. It's exactly the life that you see when you close your eyes and you envision how things can be better than how they're currently going right now. It's the way that you feel when you see that picture or movie in your own mind. If you can see it, you can be it. This just means that if you can honestly and mentally observe yourself achieving a goal and feeling the emotion that you would feel if the goal were achieved, then you increase your chances of actually achieving it just by visualizing it.

Of course, if you're visualizing yourself, for example, winning the Olympics in diving, you will also have to be practicing the skills that can get you there because visualization in itself is not magic. It's just the beginning of creating that dream life and it's what will carry you through.

Thinking about the dream life I was creating, I could envision what my gym looked like. I could see the sun shining through in the morning and a hot cup of coffee awaiting me afterwards. I could see my kids playing in the other room and us sitting down to enjoy breakfast as a family. All the parts of my dream life were crystal clear in bright colors.

Where to Start

You've probably done visualization and you don't even know it. Maybe you've done it in the shower and just mindlessly visualized what you didn't want your day to look like and what you did want your day to look like. You're washing your hair and you see it happening like a movie in your mind.

Another way that you can practice visualization is while driving. You don't have to close your eyes to visualize things. It's just creating a picture in your mind. So you can be completely and totally aware and awake, but you're consciously thinking about your dream and feeling how it feels to live it out.

You can also wake up early and do a meditation practice. You can take part in hypnosis and hypnotherapy (which spoiler alert, is just meditation with a goal. How perfect!). You can do visualization through EFT (Emotional Freedom Technique) or AFT (Aroma Freedom Technique). There are so many ways to access and solidify your dream life in your mind.

I mentioned AFT so I want to touch on aromatherapy for a minute. This is the aromatherapist in me wanting to share all the amazing benefits of essential oils. Our sense of smell is our only sense that's directly connected to our limbic system in our brain, where our emotions, memory, sleep, and hormones are regulated. So, if you practice meditating with a bottle of lavender essential oil, and you do that consistently over time, when you're out in the garden and you smell lavender, it's going to connect you to that memory without you even knowing that it happened because, as mentioned, your sense of smell is directly connected to your memory system. So pulling all these different things together with your visualizations will make things easier for you and will allow you to be able to do it and feel it at any moment.

If you want more help with visualization, there will be a section at the end of the book where we'll give you more resources and places to go to get help with all of the content of this book, including visualization.

Tips to Enhance

This is your homework assignment. Consider the following questions when working through your visualization. What do you see? Hear? Feel? Both tactile and emotionally? What do you smell? What do you taste? Let's talk through your example.

Here's an example of this practice. I have this dream of buying a beach house on the ocean. In my mind, I can see the sheer curtains blowing in the wind when the windows are open. I can feel the soft, warm breeze on my arms. I know exactly the temperature. I can smell and taste the salt in the air and I can see myself smiling, cozied up with a book in the corner of the room. This vision lives so deeply inside of me, that I can call on it at any moment and it feels like I'm literally living there. What can you create to call on at any moment and eventually live fully?

Chapter Nine

WRITE YOUR OWN DAMN RULES

I had been waiting for $10K months as an entrepreneur because that's what I believed would prove that I had made it, that I was successful. This was a goal I had written on my dream board for years. People were selling courses on how to make 10K months and coaches were making promises to get you there. Until I hired a coach and he asked me why I hired him. I told him I wanted to be successful. He asked, "What does that mean?" And I replied, "Making 5-digit paychecks monthly." "Who made that rule?" he said. "Who says that 10K months equal success?"

"Umm, everyone?" I replied.

Wrong.

Then he completely changed the way I thought about my life when he said, "No one can write your rule book except you. YOU decide what success means for YOU. This is your life and you get to write your own damn rules. What if you wrote the rule that every day your feet hit the floor upon waking is a successful day?"

And so I did. Imagine the mindset shifts that happen when you do that. Imagine the growth you create in your beliefs and the gratitude in your entire being.

I am successful every day my feet hit the floor. After that, anything I do is a bonus!

Here's where I see most people holding themselves back in life. Guilty as charged myself! We hold ourselves to some standard that someone else created. We try to do the things everyone else is doing, or what we believe everyone else is doing, or what social media makes it look like everyone else is doing. And whether you believe it or not, as soon as you let that go, you open up more possibilities than you can imagine.

You should try it just to see, re-write your rules for YOU and no one else and see what happens. It doesn't have to look anything like mine, or it can, up to you.

All We Have is a Vase Full of Skittles

Alright so, cool, you wrote new rules for your life. And I know what you're thinking, setting rules does not equal money coming in, you still have to live, right?

Yes. Writing your rules is just the first part. It's the building block to the life you're creating. Quite literally the ground rules.

But have you noticed how when you ask people how they're doing, they'll often reply "busy!"? What does that actually mean? Busy having fun? Busy cooking? Busy landscaping? It's become this catch all term and it basically means "I just don't have time to tell you what's taking up all of my time because I'm not even sure what is" You've probably done it, I have too. It's so easy to slip into that answer. But what if you started answering "productive" instead?

The Oola guys taught me something I use every single day of my life now and it has allowed me to become productive with my day rather than busy. It's this thing called oranges and skittles and I promise you, if you implement this, you will

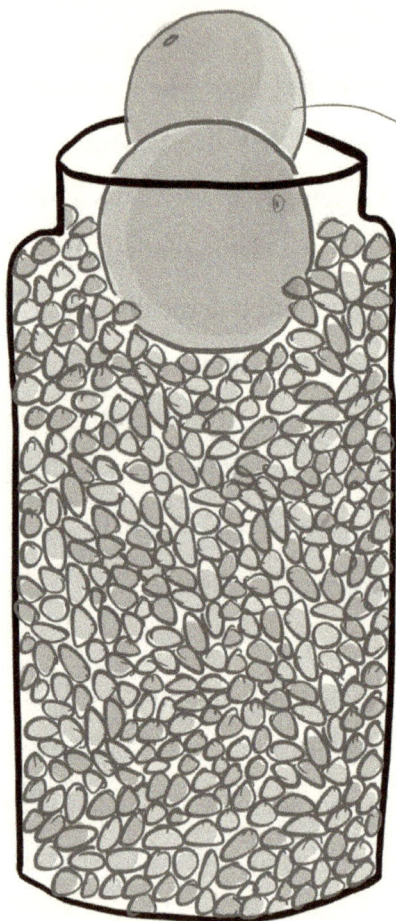

The Busy Person's Day

Oranges
Daily Action Steps aligned to your goals.

Too often they aren't prioritized & don't fit into the day.

Skittles
All the tasks in a day that need to get done but don't move you closer to your goals

achieve some major goals in the next 365 days and beyond.

Imagine that you have three oranges and a king size bag of skittles. The three oranges represent three actions steps that you will take in a day towards your big goal. So for example if your big goal was to lose 50 pounds, one action step would be to exercise 45 minutes a day, one might be to drink half your body weight in ounces of water, and another might be to eat a healthy meal three times a day. Would you agree that if you did those three things, you would be moving closer to your goal of losing 50 pounds? You might call this being productive.

Now imagine that the skittles are the everyday tasks that need to get done in order to live. Things like food shopping, laundry, pickup and dropoff, cooking, cleaning, mowing the lawn, I could go on and on. Are these things important in the day to day? Of course! Do they move us closer to our goal of losing 50 pounds? Not really, maybe one indirectly does because you can't eat if you don't food shop. But for the most part, these tasks are busy tasks.

Ok now imagine your life as a tall vase and the first thing you do is fill that vase with the king size bag of skittles. Then you try to fit the three oranges on top and realize they don't fit. Congratulations, you are busy.

Let's take everything out and try again. This time, let's prioritize our oranges and put them in first. Now let's take the king size bag of skittles and put them in. What happens? Your oranges fit and your skittles filled in the spots between the oranges. You fit both the big bag of skittles and all three oranges inside the vase.

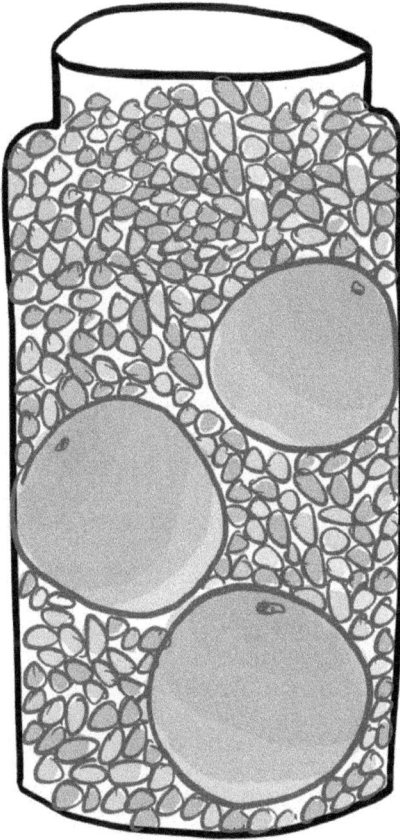

The Purposeful Persons Day

These first

Oranges

Action steps toward your goals, when prioritized, always fit into your day

Skittles

When filtered around your Oranges, still get done

That means your day was productive! You did it!!! And not only that, but you also took three steps towards a goal you are working on and have made progress. How do you think your life will feel if you prioritize your oranges every single day? What do you think you'll accomplish? My guess is a whole bunch of goals that have been only our goal list for years.

Now Apply It!

Here's the thing, most won't do it. Because it's "hard". Because our ego tries to protect us and is constantly looking for things to warn us about that are outside of our comfort zones. It will try to protect you from hurt or rejection of others. It will help you rationalize not taking action and try to keep you from experiencing new or difficult emotions. I like to turn that around and ask you how hard life will be if you don't do it. How hard would life be if you didn't lose the 50 pounds?

How hard would it be if you didn't get out of debt? How hard would it be if you stayed in that toxic job, friendship, or relationship?

Seeing the vase in my mind is a physical example that I can picture. Every day when I wake up, I think about my three oranges, and what my Skittles are that need to be done. I can fit them all in as long as I prioritize the things that move me towards achieving the life that I really want to achieve.

When I first started doing this, every night before I went to bed I would put a line down the middle of a 3 x 5 notecard and then a line across the top. On the left-hand side I would put my oranges column. On the right-hand side I would have my skittles column. I'd open up my calendar and look at the next day. What do I have going on? Okay, we have a dentist appointment. That's a Skittle because that's something that has to be done, but it doesn't necessarily push me towards my goal. I'd continue to write down all my Skittles.

Then I'd look at my oranges. I've got to read my 10 pages and work out in the morning, and I was working on (and still am) decreasing my debt so I have to log in and track my bank account and track my finances.

That note card was with me all day. If someone said, "Hey Gwen, what are your daily action steps today?" I would be able to whip out that 3 x 5 notecard and say, "Here you go. This is what I'm working on."

This is your chance in life, wherever you are right now to use the 5, 4, 3, 2, 1 Mel Robbins method and GO. Nothing in your life changes, unless you change. Program "easy" into your daily affirmations. A few of my favorite affirmations are things like:

I do [X] with grace and ease.

The life I desire is unfolding before me, and I easily flow with change.

Everything in my life flows perfectly and with ease.

The hardest part is starting, it gets easier every day after that.

Affirmations

Tear along dotted line

Getting Stuck on Goals

When it comes to setting goals, there are a few things I see people getting hung up on all the time.

When Goals Are Too Big?

I see this all the time with either income or debt payoff. Let's say you pick a goal to pay off $100K in debt in 12 months. This is totally a possibility, but if you don't give yourself little wins along the way, it will be very hard to stay consistent for 12 months. I like to help my clients break down their big goal into smaller goals to be able to allow themself quick wins. Quick wins boost your endorphins and tell your body to keep going because it gets rewarded with wins along the way.

If you've never paid down debt you're going to want to break that big goal down into ten, $10K chunks. And maybe, whenever you hit a 10K chunk and you can successfully cross it off, you can incentivize yourself with a date night, or something you enjoy. It's just simply breaking it down into small chunks that over time, will add up to achieving that big goal.

My Daily Steps Don't Look the Same

A weight loss goal might have similar goal steps everyday – hydrate, sleep eight hours, eat three healthy meals each day. But it might also be that your daily action steps look different.

For example, one of my goals is to be completely debt-free minus our mortgage. Now that's a huge goal. I'm giving myself time to create that goal. But what are some daily things that I can do that keep myself on track? Well, the last day of the month is probably going to look different than the first day of the month so I might set action steps on the last day of the month to calculate a new budget for the coming month, make sure all bills are paid and transfer my extra income to my investments. On the first day of the month my action steps might look like posting the budget where I can see it, checking in with my spouse about the upcoming month, and logging into my bank account.

See how all those action steps are important and they change throughout the month? Don't get caught up in having the same daily goal steps every single day. But know that each step is intended to move you towards achieving that long-term goal so make sure it does that.

Why Not 30 Oranges?

Show me a "to-do" list and I'll show you someone who loves checking things off. But that's not what this is about. So why three oranges, not thirty?

Now say that you're a human that has a job and you work eight hours a day. Maybe you've got kids at home and you like to eat. There's just not enough time in a day to achieve 30 daily action steps. You'd give up on day two. So, three daily action steps is a good balance to your day that also contains skittles in between.

As long as you don't make the oranges too grandiose, you'll accomplish them. Trust me, the first time you forget to do all three and then at 10pm realize you haven't done them will be the last time you do that. No one wants to be doing all three of their action steps at bedtime. If you achieve your goals, you're more likely to get up tomorrow and try the same thing. If you have 30 written down and you accomplish 10 of them, you'll look at your list at the end of the day and say, "Ok, I missed twenty action steps so tomorrow I'll do my 30 plus the 20 for a total of 50 action steps." I mean, you'll get really far behind really fast and lose interest in doing any of them. It's just not fair to expect your brain and your body to be able to accomplish that much in a day.

Those oranges usually require mindset work. Grocery shopping is easy, you can probably do it with your eyes closed. But to create new habits so that you can work towards achieving a big goal, that takes a lot of mental space.

So remember, "quick wins" makes it easy for you to create habits. Three to five oranges every day will give you "quick wins" so you'll get that satisfying feeling of accomplishment and you'll want to show up each day.

Celebrate Success

Remember, you write the rules. Don't be so hard on yourself. Celebrate another day lived, another day working towards this new life you're creating by design, not default. The more you learn to celebrate you, the easier your path will be.

We're All Vibin'

We've all walked into a room where there were two people who had just been arguing. How could you tell? Most people would say "it just feels off". What you're feeling is the energy they put out in their words, their body posture, their thoughts and their emotions.

There's some irony in my life and career here. It's no coincidence that I studied sound waves and frequency in graduate school. Let's look at how sound travels so we can better understand measuring other types of energy.

The way that sound works is that it's a vibration, and it's measured in frequency or cycles per second. So imagine a sound entering your ear canal. It hits your tympanic membrane, which is kind of like a big trampoline, causing a vibration which then moves the three smallest bones in your body called the ossicles. These bones are set into motion which moves fluid inside the cochlea stimulating hair cells inside the inner ear. All of these hair cells are receptor cells responsible for certain frequencies in our hearing and sound gets sent to the brain.

Now, in the day to day you probably don't think about that whole process. You pick up a phone, you talk to somebody and you hear the sound of their voice. You don't think about how sound is actually working. And we can't see the frequencies - it's not visual, yet we understand that it's a frequency and energy. Our bodies, and all living things around us, also have energy and vibration that can be measured (frequency), but for some reason humans have a hard time understanding that even though we can't see the vibrations of that feeling or thought, it still has a measurable frequency.

In fact, the word emotion is actually "e motion". It's energy in motion. Below is a picture of the human body with all the organs and frequencies

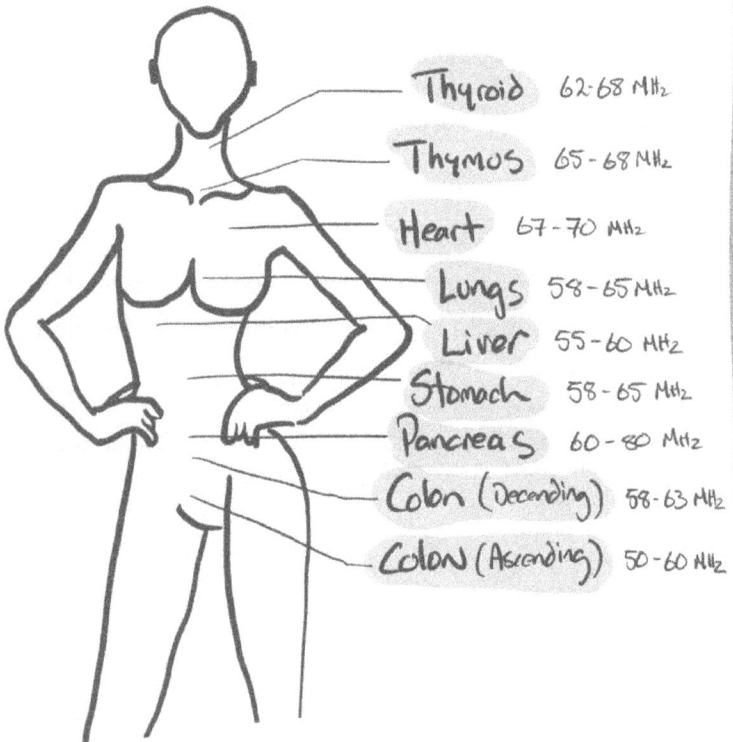

BODY ORGAN FREQUENCIES

Thyroid 62-68 MHz
Thymus 65-68 MHz
Heart 67-70 MHz
Lungs 58-65 MHz
Liver 55-60 MHz
Stomach 58-65 MHz
Pancreas 60-80 MHz
Colon (Descending) 58-63 MHz
Colon (Ascending) 50-60 MHz

that each organ has, along with pictures of emotions - like the emotion of joy and its frequency, sadness and its frequency, etc. and you can easily see how everything we encounter has measurable energy and how everything is connected.

What do you think will happen if you tell yourself you can't complete a goal, or a goal is too hard, or you constantly think you're not worthy of living the life you dream of? Your energy will be negative and every thought you have will bring the frequency of your cells in your entire body down. Do you know what happens to cells that function at this level of frequency for long periods of time? They create physical problems in the body. And when physical symptoms start showing up, it's the body yelling at you for missing the emotional and spiritual signs that tugged at you prior. This is exactly how I ended up in Adrenal Fatigue. Stress lead to internal inflammation, internal inflammation lead to headaches, poor sleep, low sex drive, and so much more.

"Technology isn't going to shift the problems we have in society and the planet—it's going to take a shift of consciousness for that to happen." - Rollin McCraty, Ph.D.

The kicker is, its cumulative so the earlier you can catch it, the easier it will be to improve it.

It's not so important to know what your frequency number is, rather how you feel physically, emotionally and spiritually. And making this check-in daily with your mind and your body will help you succeed in your day. Do you notice that you're feeling low today? Or maybe exceptionally good. The aim is to vibe high every day because when you vibe high, you feel really good, you're healthy, you're happy, and your emotions are in check. So just knowing how to tune in to how your body feels is important for knowing when and how to change it.

VIBRATIONAL FREQUENCY Chart

UNCONDITIONAL LOVE
PEACE
JOY
GRATITUDE
KINDNESS
ENTHUSIASM
OPTIMISM
HOPE
CONFIDENCE
CONTENTMENT
INDIFFERENCE
APATHY
ANNOYANCE
WORRY
ANXIETY
SADNESS
JEOLOUSY
ANGER
DESPAIR
GUILT
HATRED
FEAR

Very High frequency

Very Low frequency

Keep Your Frequency to Yourself

Now that you know what to look for in your own body and you know that you can control your own

vibe or measurable frequency, what happens when people around you don't?

For over a century, scientists and doctors have been measuring the bio field of the heart aka how far the heart's energetic reach is outside someone's body. What's been found over time is that the heart actually sends more signals to the brain than the brain sends to the heart every day. In fact, every time the heart beats, it sends out a magnetic field and the heart's magnetic field reaches every cell in the body. The heart's electrical field is 60 times greater than that of the brain's electrical field and can be measured ten feet away from the body.

So the next time you enter a room where two people have been arguing, you understand why you can feel the negative energy. We can't control everyone else, but we can certainly control the vibe we have and the vibe we give off.

Vibe Daily

Here are a few ways that you can guarantee a high vibe daily:

- Be around people who are positive and who enhance your life.

- Be in situations that are positive.

- Eat healthy foods that nourish your cells in your body

- Drink lots of water

- Meditate daily

- Decide who and what you want to allow into your bubble, your aura, your space - which is your energy field surrounding your body.

- Have boundaries.

This includes family and friends. My mom used to say, "Garbage in, garbage out," which just meant what you put into your body is exactly what you're going to get out. She was talking about food. If you put garbage in, your skin is probably not going to look great. You're going to look tired and your immune system is going to be crappy. You also want to have healthy friend relationships, a healthy workspace, good health and plenty of sleep.

All these things are funneled into your body. If you put good in, you're going to get good out. That includes your frequency and your vibration.

The Outcome of Life is in Your Hands

There was a great book called, *The Secret* by Rhonda Byrne, which is about how you can

204 · DR. GUINEVERE ANNE STASIO

control your energy. What she says is that you can control the outcome of life by what you put out because what you put out, you get back. I like to do this thing when I say something or think something that's not aligned with my goals. Whenever I recognize it (which is easier to do now that I've practiced a lot), I say outloud "cancel, cancel, delete, delete," and I take back the thought. Then I think of a better thought and state it outloud in order to cancel out the original thought with a new, goal supporting statement in order to delete the original thought completely.

Replacing Bad Thoughts

You might be wondering what a goal supporting statement looks like. Let's take my money challenges for example. There were many times that I told myself I wasn't good with money. So I'd say things like "I can't get an apartment because I've never been good with money." Finally recognizing that this was a low vibe thought, I would then say, "Cancel, cancel, delete,

delete" and then replace it with "Up until now, I may not have known how to be good with money, but I'm learning how to get better at it every single day." Just transform it a little bit.

What about weight loss. If you find yourself saying you always fail when it comes to losing weight, replace it with something like "I'm not perfect but learning how to eat right and exercise is becoming easier and easier."

Recognize it, reframe it, practice it every day, and evaluate your environment and the people you surround yourself with, which is what we're going to talk about in the next chapter.

You can do this anywhere and yeah, you might get some looks for talking to yourself, but the end result is worth it because you're in complete control of the outcome of your life.

My Non-Best Friends

In high school and college I could count the amount of friends I had on one hand, and one of them was my sister. I always felt badly about myself for not having tons of friends like everyone else seemed to have. But I just wasn't the social butterfly and I didn't want to hang out in big groups of people. I labeled myself an introvert and pretty much stuck with that as my excuse.

I went on to graduate and enter the workforce, meeting a few new friends along the way that I enjoyed spending my time with. Our circle was small but consistent. We shared our woes about work during the week and went out on the weekends to forget about work. We were all just chugging along, checking boxes and following the typical work-life path. Until I wasn't. I got a glimpse of something that allowed me to start working on bettering myself (you guys know this story already!) and I ran with it. And while I was working on myself, something happened with my friends. I started to feel disconnected, I started to feel like we had less and less in common. And I started to figure out what I wanted more of and what I wanted less of in my life.

This was a hard time for me. In a space where I felt like I was finding my true self and starting to really understand who I was and what I wanted, I also felt I was losing another part of me. But the truth is, on this personal development journey the friends I had kept in my inner circle up until then were supportive of old Gwen. They didn't think my new life choices were fun or exciting and they certainly didn't want to support what I was doing. We slowly moved further and further away from each other as meetups felt forced and awkward, until I made the choice to no longer initiate the friendship.

This was the first time I ever fired a friend. But it was also the first time I respected myself enough to do so.

Your Inner Circle

Your inner circle are the people that you keep close to you. These are the people that lift you up. They're positive, you want to be around them, you never feel like you have to include them, you don't have to work for their friendship, they make you want to be better, and they're who you would call to share good news so you can celebrate together. These are people that you want to do life with.

And sometimes, you have to re-evaluate your inner circle.

I've always heard that you should have about five really close inner circle friends, and that you never want to be the smartest one in your circle. There should always be somebody smarter than you so that you can learn from them. I know what you're thinking, how does the smartest person ever find their inner circle then?! Here are my thoughts on it.

I think we all have strengths in different areas. So, you could be smarter in finances while one of your inner circle friends is smarter in health and fitness. We all have something to learn from the people we surround ourselves with. And you'll know you've got a great inner circle when meetups last forever, there's tons of conversation and question asking and you feel like you want to take notes every time you hang.

These friends will keep your brain thinking, they'll keep you motivated, and challenge you to think differently. You don't want to have everyone in your inner circle say, "Gwen, you're fantastic and I agree with everything you say." That would make you feel like you're just a preacher, like they're praising everything you say. You want to have people who disagree with you, but also are able to vocalize why they disagree with you. It's the respect of each other's opinions and the acknowledgement that neither one of you may be right, but you're right for you, and they're right for them. You don't have to have the exact same opinion for someone to be congruent in your inner circle. The hard part about the inner circles is that as you continue to grow, it can continue to change. But if you are willing and open to see that as an opportunity to grow with it, then it will always be a positive change for everyone involved. Oh and, your inner circle friends might also have inner circles of their own. This is fantastic because it means more opportunities for meeting like-minded people.

Just because you've had a friend since junior high, doesn't mean they are an automatic part of your inner circle. When we made friends in junior high, you weren't concerned with support or selecting friends because of their knowledge. You were only worried about who likes you and who doesn't. But as you get into adulthood, you start to realize that you might not want someone in your life anymore. It's not a mean-girl thing, it's just that you want to make sure you're living life for you, and if they're not one of your biggest supporters, why would you want them in your inner circle? You have to be really selective about who you let in.

So what about acquaintances or work friends? These are people you have to be friendly with, but it doesn't mean they get to be in your inner circle if you don't want them to be. Same goes for family! You may not necessarily select them as a friend, but you can't really exclude them entirely from your life because you work with them or they are relatives and it's important to keep a good relationship with these people. This is where really good boundaries come in. You get to decide how much time you spend with them and how much you let their opinions and words affect the way you live your life. Because you know everyone wants to give you their opinion. And if they're not somebody you'd include in your inner circle, you can politely thank them for their thoughts and then choose not to do anything with it and you don't even have to let them know. So create boundaries around who you want in your life and who's in your life because they have to be, and know how to navigate the difference.

Inner Circle and Values

Here's where you get to do some thinking about who you want in your inner circle. Maybe you read the above text and you started thinking about why you keep certain people around if they don't bring value to your life and maybe you started thinking about who you do want in your circle.

How do you know it's a good fit? I'd say one general characterization of someone you want in your inner circle is someone who challenges you and also doesn't talk shit about you. All kidding aside though, what types of things should you be looking for in your inner circle friends? Well, these people are probably going to share a lot of the same values that you share. We talked about values a few chapters back so now you are probably really clear on what you value in life. And once you realize what your values are, you might find it easier to see now that the people you were keeping close to you before don't share the same values and that's why you have drifted apart. This could be complete clarity for you! I know when my original inner circle of friends started to feel forced and weird, I got really upset. I didn't understand why or what changed. Maybe you've been having a hard time with one of the people in your circle. We've all had that friend where it doesn't feel like things are being reciprocated or it feels like we're putting in all the effort to make the friendship work. Well, now that you're clear on your values, you can realize you probably have both grown and that it is ok to decrease the amount of time or effort you spend with that friend.

Again, your inner circle should consist of people with the same values; people who want to improve their life and people who aren't negative all the time. They should be people who see the light, who aren't always complaining or constantly negative because remember, your vibe is affected by their vibe.

So look for friends with good vibrations that are emotionally healthy or willing to grow and learn. These are people who have something to share and want to share it with others. People who support you and understand you and want to grow with you. These people will raise your vibrations and make you a better you.

The thing is, I had to better myself first before I could find my right people so if you don't know who yours are yet, that's ok! Sometimes we have to grow and re-evaluate who we let enter our lives and that takes time. Our time and space is precious and you should only share it with those who have

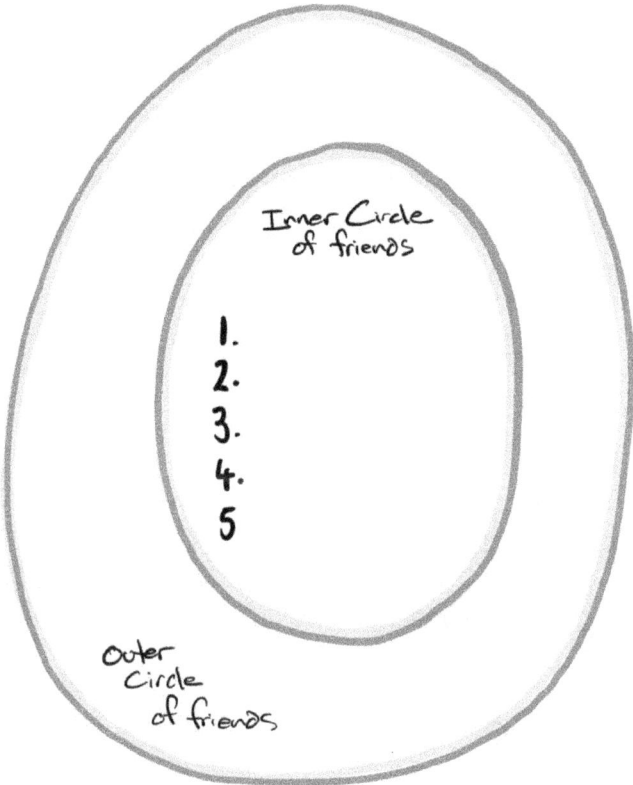

216 · DR. GUINEVERE ANNE STASIO

your best interests and want to learn to grow alongside you.

Don't Talk Shit

At some point in your life, you will have this realization that a person does not belong in your inner circle, and you need to unfriend them or stop talking to them because they're just not good for what you're trying to accomplish and who you're trying to be. Some of these friends are friends we've had in our lives for a long period of time. Maybe you've even grown up with them. It's not so easy to cut off a friendship that's been with you through thick and thin. I'm here to tell you that it doesn't have to be a swift cut off, unless you've finally realized it's toxic and your friend has got to go. At this point, there's so much history there that surely you'll want to keep checking in on this friend or see what they are doing. Resist the temptation to search for the past that once felt good but you know doesn't anymore.

It's going to be hard and they might be angry. You may even have to block them on social media so that you're not affected by their negative energy. But what starts to happen is you'll start creeping on them. You'll start wanting to know what they're up to and you might even talk shit about what you see them doing (or not doing). This happens when we feel guilty about making a decision and we just want to make ourselves feel better for it. But don't give in, just don't do it. When you talk shit you start to decrease your vibration. And then you'll be tempted to bring the conversation into your inner circle which will bring their vibration down too. Remember how we said that what you put out, you get back? If you put shit out, the shit will come back to you.

It's easy to complain. Everyone wants to complain, it's gossip and it's the fuel to many fires. I encourage you to recognize when this is happening so you can get up, go for a walk and immediately change your energy.

Homework

Your homework is to select your inner circle. Select your five best friends. Sit down and make a list of who they currently are and really look at what they bring to the table. Are they supporting you? Are they positive? Do you find that there's this one person in your inner circle who is bringing you down, always complaining and always talking negatively? Maybe you don't pick up the phone because you don't want to have that conversation. If you look at your circle and you find people like that, one of the hardest things to do is decide that you don't want to continue on with that relationship. It's not cut and dry. You can't just say, "See you later," and act like the friendship never happened. Sometimes there's going to be a conversation and sometimes you just naturally drift apart.

Who you choose to have in your inner circle is where you're choosing to spend your energy and your time, so just be really selective about the people that you want in your life because surrounding yourself with these people will make your life easier, make it better, and will make achieving your goals nearly effortless. So, pick the five best people in your life and write them down, then confirm that those five people are truly the people that you want in your inner circle going forward.

Your inner circle doesn't always know that they're your inner circle. Maybe you decide that someone you spend a lot of time with is not the best person for you to be around all the time. They're not benefiting you. You don't need to call them up and say, "Hey listen, you're out of the inner circle. You're cut out!" They don't actually need to know, you just set boundaries, remember?

When you unfriend somebody on Facebook, that person doesn't get a notification that says they are unfriended. You are just unfriending them because you've decided that that energy is not good for you and you don't want to see their posts. It's the same concept. A person doesn't need to know that you're not including them in your inner circle. You will probably just end up spending less time with them. And if you stop reaching out, you might find that they stop reaching out as well. You could just end up going your separate ways and it's not even a big deal. So, no one needs to know when they are out of your inner circle.

For me personally, I can think about one situation with a friend who had been in my life for a really long time. There were red flags along the way. I found myself complaining about our friendship more than I was excited about it. When I started to understand and realize that my energy was important and that the people that I surrounded myself with was important, it just naturally fizzled out. The communication stopped on both sides. There was no drastic unfriending or not talking anymore. It just naturally worked its way out. When a friendship naturally fizzles out on both sides, it's probably a sign that it's just not a friendship that was meant to be. It was more toxic in the end than it was beneficial. So, it's just becoming aware and bringing it into view.

We have a maximum of five people in our inner circle because if there are too many, it's almost too much for you to keep up with. Just like our daily goal steps, keep it three to five. It's a good quantifiable number that you can keep track of because you want to be just as involved in your inner circle's lives as you want them involved in yours. If you've got 25 people in your inner circle, it's not fair to you. You wouldn't be able to give the same amount of energy to all 25 people. Five is a good cushion to avoid that overwhelming feeling, but it's also enough that you've got different opinions, and you can benefit from having these different viewpoints in your life.

Maybe right now you've got a solid list of two. Perfect! Great start. If you're wanting to expand your inner circle but don't necessarily have friends you can think of who you would want to include, sit down with your current list and ask them if they have friends who they think would be beneficial to the group. Suggest a meetup or potluck dinner to meet some of them. It might take time because it takes time to get to know somebody and learn their values but it's not about rushing to find your five.

Another way to expand or replace someone is to get involved in things that you like doing. We talked about finding joy in what you love, in your creativity, in your hobbies, in the things that you like to do. Join a group and start to meet in person. If you like horseback riding, join a horseback riding group. Don't join a group just to evaluate everybody to find your next inner circle person.

It's about keeping an eye open and just being aware of who you want in your life. You'll know when you connect with somebody because you'll click in conversation immediately.

When I started to recognize that I wanted to do something different, without even knowing it I started to look around and look outside of this box that I had been stuck in for so long. I ended up buying a product that I was attracted to because I was trying to be more healthy-minded. I immediately expanded this whole view of people in my life. I saw this community of people who were working to better their lives. They were eating healthier, they were working towards big financial goals, and I started learning from them that all this was possible. Because they were vibrating higher and working together to do that, it rubbed off on me and allowed me to start vibing higher too.

I allowed myself to be open to a different energy. What can happen so often in life is that we're so used to communicating in this one little box, that we can't even physically open the door and allow ourselves to take in another area. If you can just be aware that there are other things going on outside of your little box, that awareness allows you to be open to pulling from other people's energy and allowing it to positively affect you.

Once I got into that community and I started to see that people were living the life that I wanted to live, I started really connecting with some of the women that were in there, and now they've become a huge part of my life. They're my inner circle because they lift me up. They were vibing higher and they were smarter in different areas of life that I had never been exposed to. They have taught me a lot, and now we all teach each other different things because we've all leveled-up in life.

Your Partner and Kids

Your partner and your adult kids are a part of your inner circle automatically. Let me start with your partner. This is actually really huge. Going back to when I realized my first marriage was not aligning with where I wanted my life to go, it was the first big realization that we were just friends. But, the friendship wasn't challenging me to live bigger and do better. That was a turning point in my life. I realized I needed to leave and expand and figure out what I really wanted in a partner. Your partner is a huge part of your inner circle. They should be lifting you up and supporting everything you do because hopefully you love that person and they love you back.

I've seen so often where spouses or partners don't support each other's decision to change jobs or careers. That puts a really big wedge in both your life and your relationship. Just think about how you can't talk to that spouse or partner about your work because they don't agree with what you're doing. That's 50% of your life that you can't talk about with someone you live with. It just puts a huge divide between you. So yes, your partner is a huge part of your inner circle by default; however, just remember you do have a choice in who you select or keep.

Children are a little bit different. They aren't really a part of your inner circle because you're leading by example and teaching them what they should be looking for in their inner circles. They might not realize that yet, but your example means more than anything. Once they become adults and establish themselves, they could potentially be a part of your inner circle, but of course you want them out there and doing their own thing too.

Personal Development

Personal development is working on developing and understanding your personal vision for life. It's not something that you can pass or fail, and it's not something you do once and then you're done. It's a continuous journey through life. As you unfold different parts of your life, you learn more about what you envision for your life.

I like to tell people that I was 30 years old the first time I heard the words "personal development", it literally had never been talked about before. I never heard it in school. No one ever talked about any of the resources for working on my life vision. What I discovered is so cool about personal development is that you can find it anywhere (when you're aware and looking). There's a whole personal development section at any bookstore. Go to Amazon and you'll find many personal development items there, too. It blows my mind that I didn't even know it existed until I was 30. Books, podcasts, retreats, events - personal development is everywhere. And there are free resources, resources of minimal investment like books, and resources like retreats that cost a little more but you can spend a whole weekend in Costa Rica on a retreat to work solely on you.

Personal Development changes over time based on a framework that Maslow developed called Maslow's hierarchy of needs. In this hierarchy of needs Maslow described levels that you can climb and in order to reach the next level, you would need mastery in the current level first. Maslow did clarify that you do not need 100% mastery to be able to move on, but what you'll understand in looking at this diagram is that people can get stuck at certain levels and just never move on. I actually think this is the biggest reason why people never allow themselves to move outside of their comfort zones.

Let's break down the levels:
At the bottom are the basic physiological needs – air, water, food, shelter, sleep, clothing, and reproduction - these are the basic needs of survival.

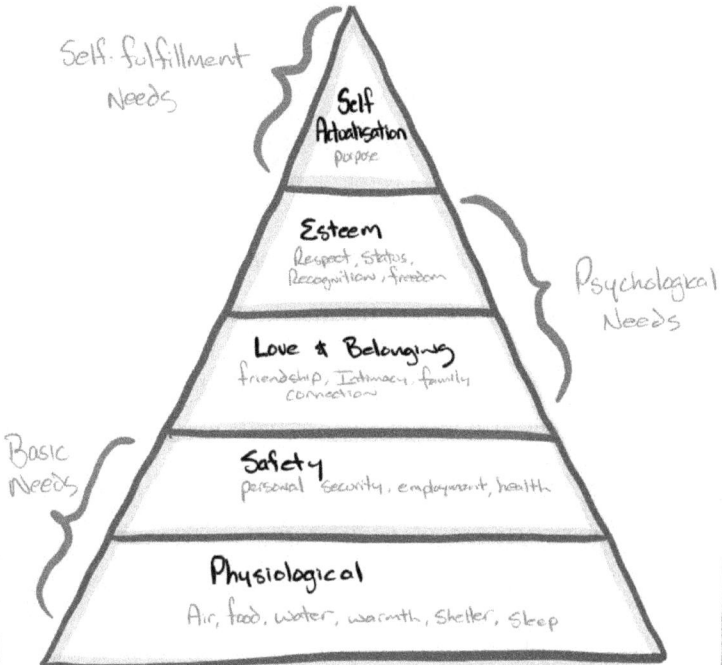

MASLOW'S
Hierarchy of Needs

Self-fulfillment
Needs

Self Actualisation
purpose

Esteem
Respect, Status,
Recognition, freedom

Psychological
Needs

Love & Belonging
friendship, Intimacy, family
connection

Basic
Needs

Safety
personal security, employment, health

Physiological
Air, food, water, warmth, Shelter, Sleep

Once you achieve that level, the next level is the need for safety and security in a physical and an economic sense – things like personal security, employment, resources, health, property. People want to experience control and predictability in their lives.

The third level of progression can then be made by satisfying the need for love and belonging.

As humans, we have a need to be loved, to give love and to belong. A lot of people search for this their entire life. This is why I believe establishing a concrete inner circle and partaking in personal development is so important.

At the fourth level there are two categories; esteem for oneself and esteem for others. Esteem for oneself looks like mastery, independence and achievement. While esteem for others looks like status or the desire for respect from others. At one time, Maslow indicated that the desire for reputation actually precedes the desire for independence and achievement and that it was more important for adolescence to achieve esteem for others before self-esteem.

The top of the hierarchy is the need for self-actualization. This fifth level relates to the need to understand. This is where curiosity comes in - your search for purpose and wanting to understand life more, having a deeper understanding for who you are, who you're meant to be, and what you're meant to do in life.

We've talked about self-worth, self-love and self-empowerment as the major components to finding our purpose in this book. Imagine what happens if someone never has a sense of belonging or never loves? They are potentially missing out on this huge part of life that leads to being the best that you can be, reaching the top of the hierarchy.

It's important to note that these needs are not hard and fast rules. While self-actualization is at the top and does allow for the most personal growth and exploration, for some the need for self-esteem might take precedence over the need to belong and so their journey to the top could look differently than others.

This chart isn't necessarily something you need to print out and hang up on your wall as a live or die, but it's helpful as you're reading this book to pinpoint where you are currently and what I'm hoping you do with the information you glean from this book, is start to take the steps into the next level of your life journey.

Mentors

When I bought those essential oils and joined the Facebook group, I started to get curious. This is where I first learned of personal development. A book had been recommended by one of the group members and up until that point, I had never read a book outside of Audiology content or cheeky love stories on the beaches of Nantucket. The book that was recommended to me was called, The Four Year Career, by Richard Bliss Brooke.

As you recall, earlier in the book I had talked about going back to work after my firstborn and having my salary reduced by $15,000. I didn't know what to do with my life. Even before reading the book though, I knew I didn't want to stay in my job forever, but I hadn't set a goal or decided what amount of time I would work there before leaving. This book then falls in my lap. I read it during my lunch hour. It's a quick read and it obviously had my attention.

This book was full of possibilities I never knew existed. I realized that accomplishing a four-year career is possible outside of what I had gone to school for. If you've never read the book, Richard helps you understand the power of residual income, and helps you build belief in not only yourself but in the Network Marketing business model as a wealth builder. It gave me the assurance that I had the capability of creating a career by helping people get healthier. As the products I was using started to help me create healthy habits and increase my vibe, I began to envision helping thousands of others too.

After reading this book I set a goal. Richard Bliss Brooke had me convinced he knew what he was talking about. He'd done it before. And he led many people to do the same thing. When my income from the side job matched my income at the office, I promised myself that I would believe in myself enough to leave my office job and work with essential oils as my "full-time" job.

It took me three years after reading the book and I was finally able to do it. I continued to follow Richard Bliss Brooke because they say success leaves clues. I listened to his podcasts. I listened to his interviews, and I read other books that he had written. I consumed all of his information. He became a mentor to me without him realizing it. But that's the reason why he writes. He knows he has information that's helpful to people, and he wants to get it out there so others can do what he did. He's actually the one who allowed me to start seeing what was possible in my life and helped me to level-up. He even took it a step further and created an interview type podcast where he interviewed top producers in my Network Marketing company and asked them questions about their journey. So not only does he leave clues, but he interviews others and pulls the clues out of them. The amount of information available to learn was endless.

So, I said Richard became my mentor, but what does that mean? A mentor is simply someone who's gone before you and done the thing that you want to do. Like me, you may not even realize you want to leave your job. I didn't know that was a path for me until I read his book. Sometimes you find a mentor accidentally. You read a book, listen to a podcast, watch a TED (Technology, Entertainment, and Design) talk, or partake in some sort of personal development, and your mind becomes open to possibilities you hadn't thought of. You can start to follow mentors who have done something that you've decided you want to do. I've been gobbling up all of Richard's information for seven plus years and through his interviews have found others who I connect with and follow too.

Oh and you're not just limited to one mentor. You can have more than one! Real-life mentors are great too. These are people you actually know and conversate with in real life. I have some real-life mentors that bring something totally different to the table that Richard Bliss Brooke doesn't bring. You will find yourself gathering clues from different people because everyone's journey is going to be a little different.

Finding a mentor starts when you begin your personal development journey. It starts with climbing that ladder of learning and getting curious about the things that you're not proficient in. You want to learn the things that you realize you don't know how to do. You can start with a Google search - "How do I leave my full-time job." You'll get a ton of resources, you'll start clicking around, and you'll read things from certain people. You're going to find the person that speaks to you.

When you start to develop yourself is when you will find your mentor.

It's important to note though that you don't have to do things exactly as your mentor did them. They will leave you clues and some of those clues will fit in your life and some won't. For example, if a mentor talks about hiring a private jet and landing speaking engagements in multiple countries to launch their book, it doesn't mean that's how you have to launch your book. But you might gain some insight on the things they talked about at their speaking engagements, or how they booked speaking engagements or what time of year they launched. Every little tidbit shared is an opportunity to apply what you learn to your situation, or not. Just don't get caught up in the comparison game.

Once my coaching clients have this realization that they're not living the life they want to live and they want to do something different, the conversation usually turns to going back to school. We still think that we need a degree or special certification in order to be "successful". I'm here to tell you that this is not true! It's possible that you'll learn more than you'll ever need to know just from your mentors and doing research on your own.

I had a friend who wanted to become a photographer. Her best friend's dad died and when she got home from his funeral, she had this huge "life is short" moment. She realized she was working in a job she didn't love and she wanted to do something else. She phoned me up and told me she was pivoting! She was going to go back to school to become a photographer. Now, I happen to know many photographers who never touched a photography class in college. Many of them watched, shadowed and listened to mentors of theirs while learning the trade themselves. They got out in the field and tried, failed, tried some more and refined their skills. None of them needed a degree to work full time as a photographer and many of them support their families with their businesses.

Now, if you decide that you want to pivot and become a surgeon or a dentist, you can't self-learn that stuff. Legally you actually have to have a degree to practice so you do need to go to school to do that. So, if you're thinking you want to pivot and do that, by all means, yes, you definitely need to go to school. But for a lot of the things that people decide they want to pivot to because it's a passion, you have to start thinking outside the box on whether or not school is necessary. I think that's where we get so hung up in life and in making changes. We think we need a certification or a degree that tells the rest of the world that we're proficient in what we're doing when we actually don't.

The lesson here is once you know that what you're currently doing is not what you want to do, check out mentors and people who've gone before you and what they have done. If they are close to you, ask them what kind of personal development journey they've gone on and what books they recommend. Every mentor will suggest somebody's book to read or someone's podcast to listen to. Start doing that deep dive and give yourself time to figure out exactly what it is you want to pivot and do.

When you begin that process is when you begin creating your dream life. You already know what you're doing is not your dream life, so give yourself a second chance. Heck, give yourself a third or a fourth or a sixteenth chance if you need to! You're not tied to anything you do unless it is bringing you absolute joy. Pivot as many times as you need to, you don't want to regret missing out on life's possibilities because you were afraid to change.

A Note About Healthy Living

I had a friend who had had a baby before me. She talked to me about how she wanted her baby's immune system to be healthy, so she got rid of toxins in her home and started to use essential oils. She told me that dryer sheets have the most toxins of any other product in your entire house. Immediately I went back in my mind to every commercial and every marketing ad for pregnant women telling you to wash all your newborn's clothes and have them ready when the baby comes home, realizing that's exactly what I had done. Now I'm thinking, "Oh my gosh! I used dryer sheets and now there are toxins on my baby's clothes and these clothes will touch her fresh new skin!" That started this ladder of learning for me about toxins and household products. I didn't know what I didn't know, but now that I knew something I needed to know more. I told my friend I wanted what she was using. So I bought some essential oils from her and began learning how to use them.

My mom still tells people to this day that it was the oils that exponentially raised my frequency and I believe it. She believes I went from introverted to extroverted-introvert because of daily consistent use. I learned how to use these oils to create a healthier home but what I really got was a healthier me (which in turn created a healthier home). They changed my overall baseline frequency for sure.

Essential oils change the way you think, they change your cells, and they change how your immune system functions. Just by using them, I started to increase my vibe which attracted more high-vibe people to me and a more high-vibe lifestyle. It's no coincidence that all these decisions came together to work in unison so if you're looking for a way to "hack the system" or get a head start, I'd start there.

Conclusion

It is true what they say, that life can happen TO you if you're not paying attention. I hope this book can serve as your wake up call to dive deep into who you truly are and what you truly want from life. The truth is, most people won't because they are afraid to show up 100% as themselves for fear of looking stupid, looking different or failing at what they set out to do. But what I've seen in coaching clients and in my own life too, is that the ones who allow themselves to be vulnerable, realize that their flaws actually make them *more* attractive. And no one is paying as much attention as we think they are to us.

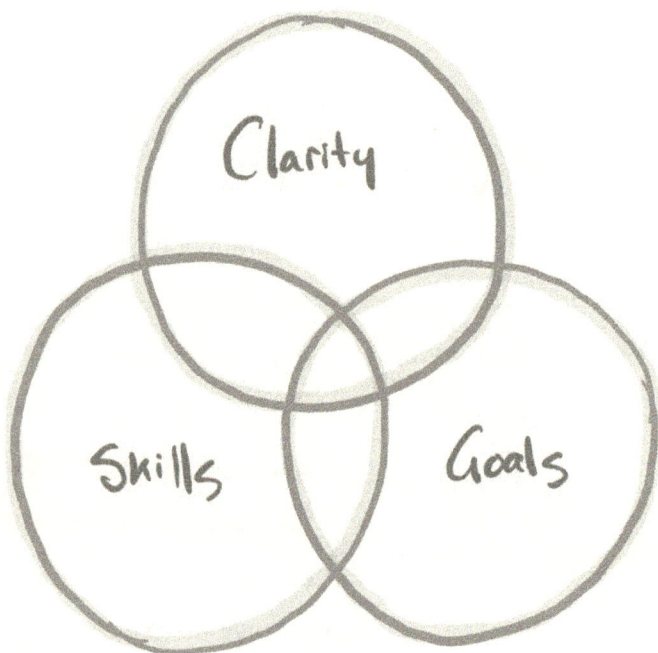

Your simple path in pivoting to your purpose and what I hope you take away from this book starts with developing clarity around who you are and what you want to do in this world. Then you can begin setting your goals around your newfound clarity and taking time to learn the skills you need to achieve them. One without the others won't get you very far, but together they allow you to create your dream life.

So here's to rocking your flaws because the fear of pivoting never really goes away, instead we just gather the skills and tools necessary to help us better work through the fear each time.

When you put your foot down and you say "I'm ready to find my true self and design a life I love!", you'll find that you create more trust with the people around you, you give others permission to show up authentically, you'll start to realize you don't need validation for your thoughts or actions, more opportunities will naturally come your way and you'll connect with people who complete your circle.

I'll leave you with this. We don't know when our last day will be. It's not morbid, it's just truth. And I wasn't joking when I said I wanted you yelling "YOLO!" on your way out. A palliative care nurse who counseled the dying in their last days revealed the most common regrets we have at the end of our lives. She outlines them in her book called 'The Top Five Regrets of The Dying' and I want to share them with you. Her patient's said:

1. I wish I'd had the courage to live a life true to myself, not the life other's expected of me.
2. I wish I hadn't worked so hard.
3. I wish I'd had the courage to express my feelings.
4. I wish I had stayed in touch with my friends.
5. I wish that I had let myself be happier.

My wish for you is that you don't have any of these regrets when you get to the end of your life.

Contact Me

If you've decided you're ready to take action and you loved what you read in this book, I am a certified life coach with a specialty in finances and I would love to help you navigate the waters. One of my biggest passions and desires in this world is to help people see that they can dream their life into existence. I do that by taking people through personalized life coaching.

You can reach out to me at
guinevere@roilhighness.com

Use this free guided visualization created for you to help you solidify your dream life:
https://roilhighness.com/landing/dream-life-visualization

Please don't sleep on the free community available to you! This sacred space at

http://www.inspiredandready.com

that I created for you is a great place to start and get plugged in with other people who are looking to change their lives and there are tons of free resources. There's a lot of content that will make you think and lots of information that will open your eyes up if you're not sure what you want to do yet. You'll find other women who are working towards achieving life by design, not default and in my opinion, that's the best life there is.